URDU
Urdu–English English–Urdu Dictionary & Phrasebook

compiled by
Nicholas Awde

little =

HIPPOCRENE BOOKS INC
New York

Thanks to Fred J. Hill, Nathaniel Karim, Sabiha A. Khan, Thea Khitarishvili and Nicholas Williams for their help in compiling this volume during its latter stages.

Typeset & designed by Desert♥Hearts

ISBN 0 7818 0970 3

For information, address:
HIPPOCRENE BOOKS, INC.
171 Madison Avenue
New York, NY 10016
www.hippocrenebooks.com

Printed in the United States of America

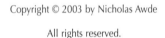

CONTENTS

INTRODUCTION

Urdu is the national language of Pakistan and one of the official languages of India. There are also Urdu speakers in the neighboring regions of Afghanistan, Nepal and Bangladesh, as well as millions of other South Asians who emigrated from the Indian subcontinent to other parts of the world. In all, some 50 million people speak it as a first language, and millions more as a second language.

Forged by history

With Urdu, several great historical strands have been brought together and woven into a wonderfully unique and colorful language. Urdu evolved many centuries ago from the original language that was spoken in the region of Delhi. Known as **Khaṛi Bolī**, or "Established Speech," this was the ancestor of both modern Urdu (**Urdū**) and Hindi (**Hindī**).

A turning point came after the invasion of northern and central India, to which Pakistan once belonged, by Muslims from the northwest in the eleventh century. These new invaders, who eventually established local dynasties in the region, brought with them not only Islam, which in time would be adopted by large numbers of the population, but also two major linguistic influences, Arabic and Persian, both of which embraced the realms of higher learning and culture.

Muslim Indians knew Arabic through the Quran, the holy book of Islam. Meanwhile,

Persian was the principal administrative and literary language. Soon Persian and Arabic words began to filter into the regional language of the historic capital Delhi and, in time, a written form using a unique combination of Arabic and Persian script was developed.

The powerful Mughal dynasty, who in the sixteenth century united the whole of northern India/Pakistan under Muslim rule, brought with them a passionate love of poetry composed in the courtly language Persian. Their patronage gave rise to a dazzling tradition of both Iranian and Indian poets, the latter lending Persian literature a unique style of its own.

Language of poets

During the course of its history, Urdu had been referred to by various names including Hindu and Rekhta, but the language eventually took the name **Zabān Urdū-e-Mu'alla**, meaning "the speech of the Royal Army Camp," in reference to the imperial army headquarters that was permamently based at Delhi. (The word "**urdū**" is derived from the Turkish word meaning "barracks" or "army," from which the English word "horde" originated.)

In the eighteenth century, Urdu, which in its spoken form had acted as a lingua franca, also began to bloom as an alternative language in which to write poetry. It was a period that saw some of the greatest Urdu poets such as Sauda and Mir, both of whom were born in Delhi, and towards the end of the century Urdu had replaced Persian as the main vehicle for Muslim literature.

Throughout the first half of the next century, Urdu continued to flourish. It was to this period that Ghalib, one of the major world poets, belonged. Although the mid-nineteenth century saw the fading of this golden age of Urdu poetry, the arrival of the first Urdu printing press saw new developments in prose and the creation of innumerable newspapers and magazines. Under British rule, English replaced Persian as the language of administration, but the use of Urdu was officially encouraged by the new rulers.

Voice for a nation

After the Partition of India in 1947, Urdu was adopted as the national language of Pakistan yet today it is by no means the only one spoken. For most of the population it is a second language that unifies their nation. The other principal languages are Punjabi (spoken by 50 percent of the population), Pashto (15 percent), and Sindhi (15 percent). The Urdu-speaking people who arrived in Pakistan from India in the aftermath of the Partition became known as the Mohajirs.

An important point of interest is Urdu's extremely close relationship to Hindi. Speakers of both have little difficulty understanding each other, since both are essentially regional — and now political — variants of a single language. Both languages are the same, grammatically speaking; the difference lies in their different vocabularies, owing to their particular cultural influences. Whereas Urdu is closely identified with Islam and adopted many Persian and Arabic words, Hindi has always been influenced by the Hindu religion and its traditions. In their written forms, the two are certainly very different: Urdu is written in a version of the consonantal Perso-Arabic script, while Hindi uses the syllabic Devanagari script, which is based on the ancient Sanskrit alphabet. ■

A VERY BASIC GRAMMAR

Urdu (**Urdū**) belongs to the Indo-European family of languages. Very closely related are languages such as Hindi and Punjabi, while other relatives include Persian, Pashto, and, more distantly, English, German, French, Italian and Spanish. Urdu is written in its own version of the Arabic script (see page 20).

—Structure

Like English, the linguistic structure of Urdu is basically a simple one. In word order, the verb is usually put at the end of the sentence, e.g.

Vo bahut zahīn ādmī hai.
"He is a very intelligent man."
(literally: "He very intelligent man is.")

—Nouns

Urdu has no words for "the", "a" or "an" in the same way as English does — instead the meaning is generally understood from the context, e.g. **ḍākṭar** can mean "the doctor," "a doctor" or just simply "doctor."

GENDER — As with many other languages, like Italian, German and Arabic, Urdu divides words up according to gender, i.e. whether they are masculine or feminine. This can be predictable, e.g. **ādmī** "man" (masculine) and **aurat** "woman" (feminine); or not, e.g. and **hoṭal** "hotel" (masculine)

a = *apple*. **ā** = *father*. **e** = *pay*. **i** = *sit*. **ī** = *heat*. **o** = *hotel*. **u** = *put*. **ū** = *shoot*. **au** = *oar*. **ai** = *pay*.

and **gāṛī** "car" (feminine). Sometimes gender is reflected in a word's ending: many masculine nouns end in **-ā**, e.g. **laṛkā** "boy", **beṭā** "son", while many feminine nouns end in **-ī**, e.g. **laṛkī** "girl", **beṭī** "daughter".

PLURALS — There are a variety of forms for the plural in Urdu, although these are usually predictable. Some involve a simple change of ending, e.g. **laṛkā** "boy" → **laṛke** "boys," **laṛkī** "girl" → **laṛkīāṅ** "girls," **aurat** "woman" → **aurateṅ** "women," while others have different forms, e.g. **masala** "problem" → **masā'il** "problems," **xātūn** "lady" → **xavātīn** "ladies". Some don't change at all, e.g. **ādmī** means both "man" and "men", **ghar** means "house" and "houses".

CASE — In addition to the plural, nouns (and adjectives) in Urdu also add an extra ending* with grammatical function that depends on conditions such as the position of a word in a sentence, whether it refers to the past or present tense, or whether a postposition (see page 11) is present.

This is generally predictable, is triggered by grammar rules only, and is best left for more advanced study, but a few examples are given in the following sections.

—Adjectives

Adjectives are like nouns in that they can take the same endings. They generally come before the noun, e.g. **baṛā/baṛī** "big":

masculine	**baṛā hoṭal** "big hotel"
feminine	**baṛī gāṛī** "big car"

* Called the "oblique" case; the neutral form is the "nominative" case.

Some other common adjectives in their basic masculine singular forms are:

open **khulā**	quick **tez**
shut **band**	slow **āhista**
big **baṛā**	old **purānā**
small **chotā**	new **nayā** (*f:* **na'ī**)
hot **garm**	good **acchā**
cold **thandā**	bad **burā**
near **qarīb**	expensive **mahaṅgā**
far **dūr**	cheap **sastā**

As in the example given above for "new", adjectives that end in **-ā** change for the feminine by adding **-ī**. Adjectives that do not end in **-ā** make no change for gender, e.g. **dilcasp** "interesting", **Pākistānī** "Pakistani", and **Angrez** "British, English", and **Amrīkān** "American"**.**

Adding **be-** to an existing noun gives the meaning of "without" or "-less," e.g. **xatar** "danger" → **bexatara** "safe" (="without danger"), **ma'nā** "meaning" → **bema'nā** "insignificant" (="without meaning").

—Adverbs

Most adverbs have a single form that does not change. Some examples:

here **yahāṅ**	below **nīce**
there **vahāṅ**	forward **āge**
now **ab**	always **hamesha**
often **aksar**	today **āj**

A common way of creating adverbs from other words is by adding **se**, e.g. **tez** "quick" → **tezī se** "quickly", **xush qismat** "good luck" → **xush qismatī se** "fortunately". Another is by repetition, e.g. **āhista āhista** "(very) slowly".

Postpositions

Urdu has postpositions, where words like "in", "at" and "behind" come after the noun and not before it as in English (although remember that you can say "who *with*?" as well as "*with* who?" – and there's no change in meaning). They generally take the oblique case:

par on; at
meṅ in; among
ke sāth with
ke ba'd after
se from; by
ko to; for
tak up to
se pahle before
ke biare meṅ about

e.g. **laṛkā** "boy", **laṛke ko** "to the boy"; **laṛke** "boys", **laṛkoṅ ko** "to the boys".

"OF" — **Kā/kī/ke** is used where English would use "-'s" or "of", e.g. **ḍāktar ki gāṛī** "the doctor's car" or "the car of the doctor." Two things happen grammatically with **kā**: first, like a postposition, it triggers the oblique case for the noun that comes before it; and second, like an adjective, it changes form according to the gender, number and case of the word following it, e.g. **laṛke kā nām** "the boy's name", **laṛki kā nām** "the girl's name", **laṛke kī kitāb** "the boy's book", **laṛki kī kitāb** "the girl's book", **laṛke ke dost** "the boy's friends".

Pronouns

Basic forms are as follows:

SINGULAR	PLURAL
I **maiṅ**	we **ham**
you *singular* **tū**	you *plural* **tum**; *polite* **āp**
he/she/it **ye/vo**	they **ye/vo**

When **ye/vo** mean "they", **log** ("people") can be added to reinforce the plural sense, e.g. **ye log, vo log**. You also sometimes find **ham log** (literally: "we people") as a reinforcement of **ham** "we".

"YOU" — **Tū** corresponds to the English "thou" and is rarely used in everyday conversation. **Tum**, technically a plural form, corresponds to the English "you" in that it can be used for when addressing one or several people. It is used in informal situations or with people perceived as having lower status than you. For politer or more formal circumstances **āp** is used, and the form is therefore the more convenient — and the most recommended — for every occasion. If you then want to make it clear that you are speaking to more than one person, you use **āp log** (literally: "you people").

POSSESSIVE PRONOUNS — These have modified forms which agree like adjectives with the gender of the person or thing possessed:

SINGULAR	PLURAL
my **merā**	our **hamārā**
your **terā**	your **tumhārā; āp kā**
his/her/its **is kā; us kā**	their **in kā; un kā**

e.g. **merā bhā'ī** "my brother", **merī bahin** "my sister", **mere vālidain** "my parents".

Demonstratives — In Urdu demonstratives are simple and do not change for gender or number:

ye this; these **vo** that; those

—Verbs

Verbs are very easy to form, adding a number of prefixes and suffixes to the basic verb form. In fact the underlying structure of Urdu verbs shares sim-

a = apple. **ā** = father. **e** = pay. **i** = sit. **ī** = heat. **o** = hotel. **u** = put. **ū** = shoot. **au** = oar. **ai** = pay.

iliar concepts to those of the majority of European languages and so its system of regularities and irregularities will soon appear quite familiar.

Every Urdu verb has a basic form that carries a basic meaning. To the end of this are added smaller words or single vowels that add further information to tell you who's doing what and how and when, e.g.

kar "do'
karnā "to do'
maiṅ karūṅ "I may do'
maiṅ karūṅ gā/gī "I (*m/f*) shall do'
maiṅ kartā/ī hūṅ "I (*m/f*) do'
maiṅ kar rahā/ī hūṅ "I (*m/f*) am doing'

You'll notice from some of these forms that distinctions between masculine and feminine are made. Like nouns and adjectives, Urdu also keeps a strict distinction between masculine and feminine in both singular and plural forms of the verb, although this is not always expressed across the various tense forms.

Some verbs, paralleling those in European languages, have different forms in some tenses, e.g. **ḏenā** "to give" → **maiṅ ḏūṅ** "I may give".

"Not" is **nahīṅ**, e.g. **Maiṅ gosht nahīṅ khāta.** "I don't eat meat" (literally: "I meat not eat."). **Mat!** "don't!" is used with commands, e.g. **rukye!** "stop!" — **mat rukye!** "don't stop!", **fikir mat kaṛye!** "don't worry!" Sometimes you'll hear **na...!** used instead in politer situations.

—Essential verbs

The most useful form of the verb "to be" you'll need is the simple present:

SINGULAR	PLURAL
maiṅ hūṅ I am	**ham haiṅ** we are
tū hai you are	**tum ho; āp haiṅ** you are
ye/vo hai he/she/it is	**ye/vo haiṅ** they are

e.g. **maiṅ ḍākṭar hūṅ** "I am a doctor", **ham Pākistānī haiṅ** "we are Pakistanis".

The verb "to have" is expressed in a variety of ways using the verb **honā** and a noun plus **kā** or a simple possessive adjective, e.g.

Aslam ke cār bacce haiṅ.
"Aslam has four children."
(literally: "Aslam's four children are.")
Mere cār bacce haiṅ.
"I have four children."
(literally: "My four children are.")

PRONUNCIATION GUIDE

Urdu letter	Urdu example	Approximate English equivalent
a	**axbār** "newspaper"	***a**pple*
ā	**āj** "today"	f**a**ther, *as in Southern British*
b	**bāzār** "market"	***b**ox, "light"*
bh	**bhā'ī** "bother"	***b**ox, "breathed"*
c	**cā'e** "tea"	***ch**urch, "light"*
ch	**chuṭṭī** "holiday"	***ch**urch, "breathed"*
d	**duniyā** "world"	***d**og, "light"*
dh	**dhūp** "sunshine"	***d**og, "breathed"*
ḍ	**ḍāktar** "doctor"	*like* **d**, *"flapped"*
ḍh	**ḍhā'ī** "two and a half"	*like* **ḍ**, *"breathed"*
e	**ek** "one"	*between* p**e**t *and the* **a** *in* pa**i**d
f	**fuṭbāl** "soccer"	***f**at*
g	**gosht** "meat"	***g**ot, "light"*
gh	**ghar** "house"	***g**ot, "breathed"*
ğ	**ğair mulkī** "foreign"	*see page 18.*
h	**hisāb** "bill"	***h**at*
i	**idhar** "(to) here"	s**i**t
ī	**vakīl** "lawyer"	h**ea**t
j	**jahāz** "ship; plane"	***j**et, "light"*
jh	**jhīl** "lake"	***j**et, "breathed"*
k	**kālij** "college"	***k**ick, "light"*
kh	**khānā** "food"	***k**ick, "breathed"*
l	**log** "people"	***l**et*
m	**mashriq** "east"	***m**at*
n	**naqsha** "map"	***n**et*
ṅ	**hāṅ** "yes"	*like* **n**, *"nasalised"*
o	**do** "two"	*between Southern British* c**o**t *and* h**o**tel

c = *church.* **ṅ** = *sing.* **x** = *loch.* **ğ/q** *see p18.* **bh/ch/dh/ḍh/gh/kh/ph/ṛh/th/ṭh** = *breathed.* **ḍ/ṛ/ṭ** = *flapped.*

p	**polīs** "police"	***p**et, "light"*
ph	**phūl** "flower"	***p**et, "breathed"*
q	**qīmat** "price"	*see page 18.*
r	**roz** "day"	**r**at, *but "rolled" as in Scottish English*
ṛ	**gāṛī** "car"	*like **r**, as in U.S. English*
ṛh	**paṛhnā** "to read"	*like **ṛ**, "breathed"*
s	**sinemā** "cinema"	***s**it*
sh	**shehar** "town, city"	***sh**ut*
t	**tārīx** "date, history"	***t**en, "light"*
th	**thoṛe se** "a few"	***t**en, "breathed"*
ṭ	**ṭaiksī** "taxi"	*like **t**, "flapped"*
ṭh	**ṭhīk** "exactly"	*like **ṭh**, "breathed"*
u	**Urdū** "Urdu"	p***u**t*
ū	**ūpar** "above"	sh***oo**t*
v	**vaqt** "time"	***v**an*
x	**xūb** "good"	lo***ch***, *as in Scottish English*
y	**yār** "friend"	***y**es*
z	**zabān** "language"	***z**ebra*
zh	**ṭelīvizhan** "television"	era***s**ure*
'	**ma'lūmāt** "information"	*see page 18.*

Nothing beats listening to a native speaker, but the following notes should help give you some idea of how to pronounce the following letters.

—Vowels

1) There is a degree of variation in the pronunciation of Urdu vowels. The combination **ai** is pronounced like English "p***ay***", e.g. **maiṅ** "I" (but also occasionally like English "wh***y***"); **au** is pronounced like English "***oa***r" e.g. **aur** "and" (but also occasionally like English "h***ow***"). As in English but to a lesser degree, you may also find variation

a = apple. **ā** = father. **e** = pay. **i** = sit. **ī** = heat. **o** = hotel. **u** = put. **ū** = shoot. **au** = oar. **ai** = pay.

between the written and spoken forms of Urdu, e.g. **bahen** for **bahin** "sister", **per** for **par** "on, at".

2) Where appropriate, an apostrophe is used in the transcription of this book to indicate that vowels should be pronounced separately, e.g. **bhā'ī** for **bhāī** "brother". Usually the sequence of vowels should be pronounced smoothly and without any "catch" in the breath (but see the note on **ʻ** below).

—Consonants

bh, **ch**, **dh**, **ḍh**, **gh**, **kh**, **ph**, **ṛh**, **th**, and **ṭh** are all *aspirated* or *breathed* versions of **b**, **c**, **d**, **ḍ**, **g**, **k**, **p**, **ṛ**, **t**, and **ṭ** respectively. Aspiration means that these are pronounced with a discernable, heavy puff of air, contrasting with their non-aspirated counterparts, which are pronounced far "lighter" than in English. A good comparison is the different way these consonants are pronounced in English (aspirated) and Spanish (non-aspirated). In the transcription used in this book, be careful to distinguish between **ch** (aspirated) and **c** (non-aspirated). Note also that here **sh** has the same pronunciation as in English.

ḍ, **ṛ**, and **ṭ** are all *retroflexive* versions of **d**, **r**, and **t** respectively. This means that they are pronounced with the tongue turned back to the roof of your mouth. For example, set your mouth up to pronounce a normal **d**, but then curl your tongue right up so that the bottom part of it touches the top part of your mouth. As you try to pronounce the original **d**, you will feel your tongue "flapping" forward. Retroflexive and breathed consonants are a common feature of the languages spoken throughout the Indian subcontinent. Similar forms can also exist in

American English, most commonly in the middle of words like "bi<u>dd</u>er", "hea<u>rt</u>", and "bi<u>tt</u>er", or at the ends of words like "ba<u>d</u>", "butte<u>r</u>", and "ba<u>t</u>".

ṅ indicates a nasal form of **n**, which affects vowels in a similar way to the "n" in French (e.g. "bon") or Portuguese (e.g. "Lisbõa").

ğ is pronounced like a sort of growl in the back of your throat — like when you're gargling. Frequently transcribed into English for other languages that have this sound as "gh", the German or Parisian "r" is the easy European equivalent. [= Arabic غ]

x is the rasping "ch" in German "ach", or the Spanish/Castillian "jota" in "jamás". This sound is frequently transcribed in English as "kh" (not to be confused with the breathed "k" in Urdu, **kh**). [= Arabic/Persian خ]

q is pronounced like a **k**, but right back in your mouth at the throat end. Imagine you have a marble in the back of your throat and that you're bouncing it using only your glottis, and make a **k** sound at the same time. [= Persian or Arabic ق]

‘ represents the same pronunciation of two underlying sounds: the "glottal stop" — a simple stop of the breath instead of a consonant — or a representation of the pharyngal consonant ᶜ*ain,* found in words of Arabic origin — it also occurs in Hebrew. In Urdu, when it comes before a consonant, it prolongs the preceding vowel, sometimes with a slight "creak" of breath separating the two, e.g. **ma'nā** "meaning" is pronounced "**ma-ana**," or simply "**mānā**". When it comes after a consonant, it can be pronounced as a sort of stop or catch in the flow of breath before articulating the following vowel, e.g. **qil'a** "castle" is pronounced in two distinct segments

a = apple. **ā** = father. **e** = pay. **i** = sit. **ī** = heat. **o** = hotel. **u** = put. **ū** = shoot. **au** = oar. **ai** = pay.

as "**qil-a**." Most of the time in this book, however, it is used as a (non-scientific!) convenient visual divider between vowels to aid reading, e.g. **bhā'ī** "brother", which can just as easily be written **bhāī**. [= Turkish "/Persian ء or ع]

—Spelling notes

1) In addition to the variations mentioned above, like English there are personal and regional alternations in Urdu of consonants and vowels in the spoken language which are not reflected in the formal, written language. These usually have no effect on meaning and are easily picked up once you have found your "Urdu ear."
2) In the rare cases where the letters **sh** represent the two separate sounds **s** and **h** in sequence, they are divided by an apostrophe, e.g. **Is-hāq** "Isaac".
3) Remember that **h**, as a separate letter, is always pronounced in combinations like **mashhūr** ("**mash-hūr**") "famous".
4) Consonants can be "doubled", e.g. **achchā** "good" is pronounced distinctly as "**ach-chā**".
5) Abbreviations used are: *m* for "masculine/male" and *f* for "feminine/female".

—English in Urdu

English words and expressions are especially used in Urdu — indeed, many are an integral, normal part of the everyday language. Pronunciation varies between English and Urdu, depending on the speaker and the circumstances. Don't be surprised if many Urdu speakers suddenly switch into English mid-sentence or interchangeably use English and Urdu words for the same thing. English terms are especially used in areas such as politics, science or technology, and where used in the Urdu in this book, they are given with their English form in quotation marks and should be treated and learned as any Urdu entry. ■

The Urdu alphabet

Urdu letter	Roman equivalent	Name of letter	Urdu letter	Roman equivalent	Name of letter
آ	**a, ā**	alif	س	**s**	sīn
ب	**b**	be	ش	**sh**	shīn
بھ	**bh**	bhe	ص	**s**	svād
پ	**p**	pe	ض	**z**	zvād
پھ	**ph**	phe	ط	**t**	to'e
ت	**t**	te	ظ	**z**	zo'e
تھ	**th**	the	ع	**'**	ain
ٹ	**ṭ**	ṭe	غ	**ğ**	ğain
ٹھ	**ṭh**	ṭhe	ف	**f**	fe
ث	**s**	se	ق	**q**	qāf
ج	**j**	jīm	ک	**k**	kāf
جھ	**jh**	jhe	کھ	**kh**	khe
چ	**c**	ce	گ	**g**	gāf
چھ	**ch**	che	گھ	**gh**	ghe
ح	**h**	baṛī he	ل	**l**	lām
خ	**x**	xe	م	**m**	mīm
د	**d**	dāl	ن	**n**	nūn
دھ	**dh**	dhe	ں	**ṅ**	nūn ğunna
ڈ	**ḍ**	ḍāl			
ڈھ	**ḍh**	ḍhe	و	**v, u, ū**	vā'ū
ذ	**z**	zāl	ہ	**h**	choṭi he
ر	**r**	re	ھ	**h**	do cash-mī he
ڑ	**ṛ**	ṛe			
ڑھ	**ṛh**	ṛhe	ی	**y, ī**	ye
ز	**z**	ze	ے	**e**	e
ژ	**zh**	zhe	أ	**'**	hamza

1. Since the Urdu alphabet is based on a consonantal system, note that the short vowels **a**, **o** and **u** are not normally written; **e** is also sometimes not written.
2. **Ain** and **hamza** are not normally written in the transliteration used in this book, and they are rarely pronounced in conversational Urdu.

Numbers

٠	١	٢	٣	۴	٥	٦	٧	٨	٩	١٠
0	1	2	3	4	5	6	7	8	9	10

URDU
Dictionary

In most cases, verbs are given in their simplest form, e.g. **kar** "do." To form the infinitive, add **-nā**, e.g. **karnā** "to do."

URDU–ENGLISH
URDŪ–ANGREZĪ

A/Ā

ā to come
ab now
ābādī population
abā father
ābā-o-ajdād ancestors
abhī right now; **abhī tak nahīṅ** not yet
ābshār waterfall
acānak suddenly; **acānak hamlā** raid
achchā good; fine; well; **achchā honā** healing; **achchā kar de** to cure; **sab se achchā** best
achchī tareh (se) well; fine *adverb*
adab literature
ādāb etiquette
adā kar to perform
adā-kār actor
adā-kārī performance
adālat court *of law*
adāvat feud
ādhā half
ādhī rāt midnight
adrak ginger
afsos hai! *familiar* sorry!
āg fire; **āg jalā** to light a fire
agar if; **agar mumkin ho** if possible
āge front; forwards; **ke āge** in front of; **āge nikal** to overtake
agle hafte next week
agle sāl next year
ahim important
ahmaq foolish
ahmīyaṭ importance
"AIDS" AIDS
ā'īnā mirror
aisā such
aivān parliament
āj today; **āj rāt** tonight; **āj shām ko** this afternoon; **āj subah** this morning
ajā'ib ghar museum
ajīb-o-ğarīb strange
ajnabī stranger
akelā single
aksar often
aksarīyat majority
alag ho/kar to split
alāmat symptom
ālamī "record" world record
ālāt appliances
alāva: ke alāva except; besides
albatta however
Allāh God
almārī cabinet; cupboard
ālū potato
ām normal; general; **ām samajh** common sense; **ām taur per** usually
amal-e-jarāhī operation; surgery
aman peace
Amerika America
amīr rich
amnī fauj peace-keeping troops
amnī muzākirāt peace talks
Amrīkī American
anḍā egg
andar: ke andar into

c = *church*. **ṅ** = *sing*. **x** = *loch*. **ğ/q** *see p18*. **bh/ch/dh/ḍh/gh/kh/ph/ṛh/th/ṭh** = *breathed*. **ḍ/ṛ/ṭ** = *flapped*.

andarūnī internal
andarūnī nālī inner-tube
andhā blind
andherā darkness *noun*
āṅgan yard; courtyard
aṅghūṭā thumb
aṅghūtī ring
Angrez British; English
Angrezī axbār newspaper in English
Angrezī British; English
angūr grape
āṅkh eye
āṅkhaiṅ eyes
āṅsū tears
āp you *singular*; **āp log** you *plural*; **āp kā shukriyā!** thank you!; **āp kā** your; yours *singular*; **āp ke** your; yours *plural*; **āp xud** yourself; **āp log xud** yourselves
apāhij disabled
apnā own
apne āp meiṅ ek unique
Aprel April
aqalliyat minority
Aqvām-e-Muttahida United Nations
Arab Arab
Arabī zabān Arabic language
ārām rest; **ārām kar** to rest; **ārām se** to be comfortable
ārī saw
asal origin
āsān easy
asar: ke asar meiṅ under
āsār-e-qadīma archeology
assī eighty
aslī original; real; main
āsmān sky
āspās nearby
aspirin aspirin
āṭā flour
āṭe kī cakkī mill
āṭh eight
aṭhāra eighteen
Ātish Parast Zoroastrian
atlas atlas
August August
auqāt timetable
aur and; more
aurat woman
Austrailia'ī Australian
Australia Australia
āvāz sound; voice
axbār newspaper
āxir tak throughout
āxrī final; last
āyā midwife; to arrive
āzād free
āzādī freedom
azīm great; **sab se azīm** greatest
azīyat torture *noun*
azmā'ish trial *test*

B/BH

bac to escape
bacā to rescue
bacā hūvā rest; remainder
baccā baby; child
baccā dānī womb
bacca denā to give birth
bacce children
bacoṅ kā ḍāktar pediatrician
bacoṅ kī ḍāktarī pediatrics
bād after; **ke bād** afterwards
badal to alter
bādal cloud
bādbānī kashtī sailboat
bādbānī safar sailing
bad-bū to stink
bad hazmī indigestion
bādishāh king
badlā revenge
bad-qismatī se unfortunately

a = apple. **ā** = father. **e** = pay. **i** = sit. **ī** = heat. **o** = hotel. **u** = put. **ū** = shoot. **au** = oar. **ai** = pay.

bad tamīz rude
bāğ garden; park
bağair without
bağāvat revolution
bāğī rebel *noun*
baggī cart
bahadur brave
bahāna excuse *noun*
bahār spring *season*
bāhar out; outside; **bāhar jā** to go out; **bāhār mulk kā fon koḍ** code: international code
baignī purple
bail ax
bainul aqvāmī "flight" international flight; **bainul aqvāmī "operator"** international operator; **bainul aqvāmī "phone code"** international code
baiṭh to sit
bait-ul-xalā toilet
bajā'e: ke bajā'e instead
bajrī gravel
bakrī goat
bāl hair
bal kā barash hairbrush
bāl sūkhāne kī mashīn hair-dryer
balğam cough
ballī plank
bālṭī bucket
bam bomb; **bam fī'ūz karne vāla** bomb disposal
bam-bārī bombardment
ban to become
banā to make; to create; to build; to yield
banāvaṭ form; shape; structure
band shut; blocked
band kar to close; to shut; to switch off
band; bānd dam
bandargāh port
bāndh to tie
bandūq gun; rifle
bank bank; **bank kā not** bank bill/note
bār bar; pub; **bār vāla** bartender
baṛā big; senior; grown-up; elder; **baṛā bistar** double bed; **baṛā corāhā** main square; **baṛā kamrā** double room; **baṛā pā'ip** hose; **baṛā sāhib** boss; **sab se baṛā** biggest
bāṛa barn
bāra twelve
barābar equal; level
barābrī equality
baraf ice
baraf bārī snow; frost; sleet; **Baraf bārī ho rahī hai.** It is snowing.
bar āmad export; **bar āmad kar** to export
barbād kar to destroy; to spoil
baṛe jūte boots
barf bārī *see* **baraf bārī**
barfelī freezing
baṛh to grow
bāṛh fence
baṛhā to extend; to lengthen
baṛhā'ī carpenter
baṛhat to hike; to lead
baṛī grave; serious
baṛī dāvat banquet
bārish rain; **Bārish ho rahī hai.** It is raining.
Bartāniyā Britain; England
barūd explosives
bas bus; enough; to dwell; **bas se** by bus; **bas "station"/bas aḍḍā** bus station; **bas "stop"** bus stop
bāsī stale
batā to tell; to describe

c = *church.* **ṅ** = *sing.* **x** = *loch.* **ğ/q** *see p18.* **bh/ch/dh/ḍh/gh/kh/ph/ṛh/th/ṭh** = *breathed.* **ḍ/ṛ/ṭ** = *flapped.*

batan womb
batax duck
bāt-cīt conversation; discussion; **bāt-cīt karne vālā** negotiator
bāt kar to talk; to tell
bāt nahīṅ! no problem!
baṭvā wallet
bāvarcī cook
bāvarcī xāna kitchen
bāyāṅ left side
bāzār market
beg bag
Begam Mrs
be-ghar homeless
be-ghar insān displaced person
be-gunāh innocent
behen sister
be-hoshī kī davā tranquilizer; anesthetic
behrā deaf
behrī fauj navy
behtarīn excellent
be-kār useless; trash
dull
beṅc to sell
be-rang colorless
be-rozgār unemployed
be-rozgārī unemployment
bevaqūf silly
bhāg to run; to flee
bhagvā orange *color*
bhā'ī brother
bhaiṛyā wolf
bhar to fill
bharā full
bhārī heavy
bhej to send
bheṛ lamb; sheep
bhī also; too
bhīgā wet *adjective*
bhot devil
bhūkā hungry
bhūl jā to forget
bīc middle; **bīc meiṅ** in the middle
bijlī electricity; light; **bijlī kā "adapter"** adapter; **bijlī kā "bulb"** light bulb; **bijlī kā batan** switch; **bijlī kā jhatkā** electric shock; **bijlī ke sāmān kī dokān** electrical goods store; **Bijlī kat ga'ī hai.** The electricity has been cut off.
bikhrā hūvā to scatter
bil bill
bilkul exactly
bilkul sahī perfect
billī cat
bīmār ill; sick
bīmārī illness; disease
binā without; **binā dodh kī kāfī** coffee without milk; **binā shakar** no sugar; **binā tax** tax-free
bīs twenty
bistar bed
bīvī wife
bo to sow
bohut very; many; **bohut pehle** long ago; **bohut sārā/sāre** a lot; too many/much; **bohut thoṛā** too little; **bohut ziyāda** too much; **bohut burā** terrible; **Bohut sardī hai.** It is very cold.
bol to speak; **Maiṅ Urdū boltā hūṅ.** I speak Urdu.
bol-cāl kī zabān dialect
borā sack *noun*
botal bottle; **botal kholne kī cābī** bottle-opener
brash brush
bū smell
Budh Wednesday
budh-dhū fool
bula to call

a = apple. **ā** = father. **e** = pay. **i** = sit. **ī** = heat. **o** = hotel. **u** = put. **ū** = shoot. **au** = oar. **ai** = pay.

bunyād basis; foundation
burā bad; **sab se burā** worse
burī tareh se badly
būṭ trunk *of car*
buxār fever; flu

C/CH

cabā to chew
cābī key
cabūtrā podium
cādar sheet
caḍḍī underwear
cā'e tea; **cā'e kā camac** teaspoon
cāh want; to want
cakh to taste
cakkā wheel
calā to drive
calāne vāla operator
cālīs forty
camak to flash; to shine
camcā spoon
camṛā leather
camṛī skin
cānd moon
cāndī silver
cāqū knife
cār four
cashmā eyeglasses
caṭān rock
caṭānī rocky
caṭnī chutney; ketchup
caudā fourteen
caukīdār guard
cauṛā thick; wide
caurāhā crossroads
cauthā fourth
cauthā'ī quarter; fourth
cāval rice
cehrā face
cek check
chalak to spill
channī filter
chāp to print; to publish
chāpā xāna publisher
chat roof
chaṭā sixth
chaṭāk ounce
chatrī umbrella
che six
chipkalī lizard
choṛ to leave; to quit; to release
choṭā small; young; junior; **chotā cāqū** penknife; **choṭā jangal** wood; **choṭa kamrā** single room; **choṭā qālīn** rug
chup to hide
chupā hidden
churā machete
chuṭṭe loose change
chuṭṭī holiday; leave
chuṭṭī kar to sack
cillā to shout
Cīn China
cing-gam chewing gum
cīnī sugar
Cīnī Chinese
cīnī ke bartan pottery
cīnx to cry; to weep
cipkā to stick
cirāğ lamp
cīz thing; **cīzeṅ** things
cor thief
corāha square; roundabout
corī theft
corī kā stolen
cotī peak; summit
cūhā mouse; rat
cun to choose
cūnā lime *mineral*
cūn'ṭī ant
curā to steal
curyā bird
curyā ghar zoo

c = *church.* **ṅ** = *sing.* **x** = *loch.* **ğ/q** *see p18.* **bh/ch/dh/ḍh/gh/kh/ph/ṛh/th/ṭh** = *breathed.* **ḍ/ṛ/ṭ** = *flapped.*

D/Ḍ/DH/ḌH

dabā to press
ḍabā box; can
dādā grandfather
dādī grandmother
dafnā bury
daftar office
dağā-bāz treacherous
dağā-bāzī betrayal
dağā de to betray
dahī yogurt
ḍā'il kar to dial
ḍāk mail; **ḍāk ka ḍabā** mailbox; **ḍāk tikiṭ** postage stamp; **dāk xāna** post office
ḍākā robbery
ḍāktar doctor; **ḍāktar kā āla** stethoscope
ḍākū bandit
ḍāl to pour; to put in
daldali ilāqa; daldal kā ilāqa marsh; swamp
damma asthma
dāna grain; seed
dāṅt tooth
ḍāṅt kā barash toothbrush
ḍāṅt kā ḍāktar dentist
ḍāṅt kā dard toothache
ḍāṅt kā manjan toothpaste
ḍar fear; **ḍar lag** to fear
ḍaram barrel
dar āmad import
dard hurt; pain; **dard kī davā** painkiller; **Kahaṅ per dard hai?** Where does it hurt?
dargāh mausoleum
dāṛhī beard
darja-e-harārat temperature
darmiyān between; **darmiyān meiṅ** during
darmiyāna average *adjective*
dars lecture
dār-ul-hukūmat capital city
darvāzā door
darvāze kā tāla door lock
darxāst kā fārm application form
das ten; **das sāl** decade
dastāne gloves
dastar-xān tablecloth
dastaxat signature; **dastaxat kar** to sign
dast-kār craftsman
dast-kārī handicraft
dastūr constitution
dasvāṅ tenth
daur era; period
daur-e-hukūmat reign
davā drug; medicine; medication; **davā xāna** clinic; **davā'ī kī dūkān** pharmacy
dāvat de to invite
dāvat invitation
dāxil to enter
dāxla entrance
dāxla mamnū no entry
dāyaṅ right *side*
de to give; to pay; to pass
dehāt village; **dehāt kā ilāqā** the countryside
dekh to see; to look; to watch; to check
dekhne vāla observer
Ḍenish Danish
Ḍenmārkī Dane; Danish
der to delay
der se delayed; late
desī folk
desk desk
dhāga thread
ḍhalān slope
dhamākā explosion
dhamākā-xez ashyā explosives
dhanak rainbow
dhāt metal

a = apple. **ā** = father. **e** = pay. **i** = sit. **ī** = heat. **o** = hotel. **u** = put. **ū** = shoot. **au** = oar. **ai** = pay.

dhīre slow
dhīre-dhīre slowly
dhiyān dījye! careful: be careful!
dho to wash
dhobī kī dūkān laundry
ḍhol drum
ḍhūp: ḍhūp kā cashmā sunglasses; **ḍhūp hai** it is sunny
dhūvāṅ smoke
diffā kar to defend
dikhā to show
ḍikkī trunk/boot *of car*
dil heart; **dil casb** interesting; **dil casbī** interest; **dil kā daura** heart attack
din day; **din kā vaqt** daytime
dīvār wall
do two; **do bār** twice; **do hafte** fortnight
dohrā to repeat
donoṅ both
dopehar afternoon; noon; **dopehar kā khānā** lunch
ḍor string
dost friend
dozax hell
drāma play; drama
du'ā kar to pray
dūb to sink
dublā thin; lean
dūdh milk; **dūdh vālī jānvar** mammal
dūkān shop; store; **dūkān dār** shopkeeper
dumbā lamb
duniyā world
dupaṭṭā scarf
dūr far; distant
dūrbīn telescope; binoculars
dushman enemy
dūsrā next; other; another; second; **dūsrī botal** another bottle

E

ek one; **ek cauthā'ī** one-quarter; **ek dafā** once; **ek jaisā** similar; **ek ke bād ek** one after another; **ek sāth** together; **ek taraf kā ṭikiṭ** one-way ticket; **ek ziyāda "blanket"** an extra blanket
"e-mail" e-mail
"emergency" darvāza emergency exit

F

fahrist list
faislā decision
faislā kar to decide
fan-kār artist
faraq difference
farishtā angle
farm farm
farsh floor; ground
farsh per on the floor
Fārsī Farsi
Farvarī February
farz duty; obligation
fasād riot; disorder
fasal yield; harvest
fasal kāṭnā reaping
fāslā distance
fatah victory
fauj army; military
faujī military *adjective*; soldier
faujī ṭeṅk tank
faulād steel *noun*
fe'l verb

fikir kar to worry; **Fikir mat kaṛye!** Don't worry!
fikir-mand worried
film film
filmī tehvār film festival
film-sāz filmmaker
firij refrigerator
fon telephone; **fon "operator"** telephone operator
fon kar to telephone
form bhaṛye to fill in a form
funon arts
fursat kā vaqt free time; leisure time
fūṭ foot *measurement*
fūṭbāl soccer; football; **fūṭbāl kā maic** soccer match; **fūṭbal kā meṅdān** soccer pitch
fuzūl trash; rubbish; worthless

G/GH/Ğ

gā to sing
gā'e cow; **gā'e kā gosht** beef
gā'oṅ village
gadaṛyā shepherd
gadda mattress; quilt
gadhā donkey
ğair mulkī foreign; foreigner
gais gas; **gais kā kūvaṅ** gas well; **Gais kaṭ ga'ī hai.** The gas has been cut off.
galā throat
ğaltī mistake; **ğaltī kar** to make a mistake
ğamgīn sad
gānā song
gandā dirty
ğār cave
gardan neck
gaṛī car
ğarīb poor
garm hot; warm; **garm kar** to heat; **garm havā** hot wind; **garm panī** hot water
garmī heat; **Garmī hai.** It is hot. **garmī kā mausam** summer
gas *see* **gais**
gavāh witness *noun*
gaz yard *measurement*
gehrā deep; **gehrā panī** deep water
gehūṅ wheat
gend ball
ghamanḍ pride
ghamanḍī proud
ghanā jaṅgal thick forest
ghāṅs grass
ghantā hour
ghanṭī bell
ghar house
ghar lejāne kā khāna take-away/-out food
ghaṛī clock; watch
ghaṛī-sāz watchmaker's
ghasīṭ drag
gherā ring *noun*
ghoṅsā bāzī boxing
ghorā horse; **ghur savārī** to ride a horse
ghumā to spin; to dial; to swing
ghuṭnā knee
gīlā wet
gir to fall
giraftār arrest
girjā church
giyāra eleven
ğizā diet
gobhī cauliflower
god lap
godām store; warehouse
gol goal; herd
golā shell *military*
golf golf
golī bullet; **golī mār** to shoot; **Golī mat māṛye!** Don't shoot!

a = apple. **ā** = father. **e** = pay. **i** = sit. **ī** = heat. **o** = hotel. **u** = put. **ū** = shoot. **au** = oar. **ai** = pay.

golī pill; tablet
gosht meat
gulāb kā phūl rose
gulābī pink
gul-dastā vase
gumbad dome
gum-nām unknown
gurda kidney
ğurūb āftāb sunset
ğurūr pride
guṛyā doll
ğusā anger; angry; **ğusā kar** to get angry
ğusal-xānā bathroom

H

had limit
haḍḍī bone
hādisā accident
haftā week; Saturday
haiz period; menstruation
hajjām barber
hākim monarch; ruler
hal plow; **hal nikāl** to solve
hāl present *time*; **hāl meiṅ** recently
hālāṅ ke although
hālat situation; state
halkā light *not heavy*
halkā phulkā khānā snack
ham we
ham xud ourselves
hamāra our
hameṅshā' always
hāmilā pregnant
hamlā attack; invasion
hamlā kar to attack
hāṅ yes
haṅs to laugh
haṅsī laughter
haṅsyā scythe
haqīqat fact; reality
har each; every
har cīz everything
harā green
harkat movement
haṛtāl strike *noun: from work*
hāsil kar to get
haspatāl hospital
hāth hand
hāth meiṅ lenā to undertake
hāth-pā'oṅ limbs
hathūṛā hammer
hathyār arms; weapon
havā air; wind
hava'ī aḍḍā airport
havā'ī ḍāk air mail
havā'ī fauj air force
hava'ī jahāz airplane; **Hava'ī jajāz kitne baje uṛe gā?** What time does the plane take off?; **Havā'ī jahāz "cancel" ho gayā hai.** The plane is canceled.
havā'ī maidān airfield
hazār thousand
hifāzat kar to guard; to protect
hifāzat protection; safety; security
hifāzatī pin safety pin
hifzān-e-sehat healthcare
hijje spelling
hijrat immigration
hil to move
Hindi Hindi
Hindu Hindu; **Hindū maz-hab** Hinduism
Hindustān India
Hindustānī Indian
hiran deer
hisā bit; part; portion; share; **hisā le** to participate
hisāb account; bill; mathematics
ho to be; to occur

c = *church.* **ṅ** = *sing.* **x** = *loch.* **ğ/q** *see p18.* **bh/ch/dh/ḍh/gh/kh/ph/ṛh/th/ṭh** = *breathed.* **ḍ/ṛ/ṭ** = *flapped.*

hoṅṭ lip
hosh sense
hoshyār sensible
hostel hostel
hotel hotel
huk hook
hukm de to order
hukūmat government
hunar skill
hunar-mand skilled
huqa pipe *for smoking*
huqūq rights
hurūf alphabet

I/Ī

ibārat text
ibtidā origin
idāra institute
iğvā kidnapping; hijacking; **iğvā karne vāla** kidnapper; hijacker; **iğvā kunindagān** hostage; **iğvā kar** to kidnap; to hijack; to take hostage
iğva'ī kidnapper; hijacker
ījād invention; **ījād karne vāla** inventor
ijāzat permission
ijlās conference
ilāqā area; quarter; region; territory
ilm-e-kīmyā chemistry
ilm-e-lisāniyāt linguistics
ilm-e-tibbīyāt physics
ilzām lagā to accuse
imārat building
imdād aid; relief aid
imtihān exam
inām prize
īṅdhan fuel
ingīniyar engineer
insāf justice
insān man; human being
insānī human; humanitarian; **insānī falāh** humanitarian; **insānī huqūq** human rights; **insānī madad** humanitarian aid
īṅṭ brick
internet internet
intixāb election
intizām arrangement
intizār kar to wait; **Merā intizār karye.** Please wait for me.
irāda intention; **irāda kar** to intend
Irān Iran
Irānī Iranian; Persian
is this; **is hafte** this week; **is ke alāva** in addition to this; **is ke jaisā** like this; **is līye** therefore; **is sāl** this year
Īsā'ī Christian
Īsā'īyat Christianity
ishāroṅ kī zabān sign language
ishtihār advert
iskel ruler
Islām Islam
Islāmī Islamic
ismagalar smuggler
isṭaipnī spare tire
istarī iron *for clothes*
istemāl use; **istemāl shudā** second-hand
itmenān baxsh satisfactory
itne sāre so much/many
itr perfume
ittihād unification
Itvār Sunday
ixtilāf dispute

J/JH

jā to go; to visit; **jā'eṅ!** let's go!
jab ke while; since
jabṛā jaw

jab-tak unless; until
jadīd modern
jad-o-jehad struggle
jāg to awake; **Kevin ko jagā'īye.** Please wake Kevin up.
jagā place
jaisā: ke jaisā like *preposition*
jak jack *of car*
jakeṭ jacket
jāl trap
jalā to burn; to light
jalāne kī lakṛī firewood
jald quick
jaldī hurry; early; soon; **jaldī se** quickly
jaldī-jaldī quickly; rapid
jālī counterfeit
jamā hūvā to freeze
jama kar to count
jamhūrīyat democracy
Janāb Mr
janāza funeral
jāṅc test; examination
jāne kī tarīx date of departure
jaṅg battle; war
jaṅg xatam ceasefire
jāṅgh pelvis
jangī qaidī prisoner-of-war
jāṅgia underwear
jannā to give birth
jannat heaven; paradise
jānvar animal
Janvarī January
Jāpān Japan
Jāpānī Japanese
jarāsīm germs
jārī continue
jaṛī-būṭī herb
jarāh surgeon
jāsūs spy
javāb answer; **javāb de** to answer
javān young person
javānī youth
jaz jazz
jeb pocket
jel prison
jhāg surf
jhagṛā dispute; fight; conflict
jhāṛ tree; to sweep
jharnā stream
jhaṭkā shock
jhaṭke concussion
jhel to catch
jhīl lake
jhuk to bend; to kneel; to lean
jhuṇḍ flock
jhūṭ lie
jhūṭā false *adjective*
jigar liver
jilā vatan kar to expel
jild skin
jins sex; gender
jinsī sexual
jism body
jīt to win
jo barley
joṛ to repair
joṛnā repair
jot to plow
Julā'ī July
Jumerāt Thursday
Jumma Friday
Jūn June
jūṅ louse; lice
junūb south
junūbī south(ern)
jurm crime
jurmāna fine; penalty
jurvān twins
justajū kar to seek
jūtā shoe
jūte shoes; **jūte kī dūkān** shoe shop

c = *church*. **ṅ** = *sing*. **x** = *loch*. **ğ/q** *see p18*. **bh/ch/dh/ḍh/gh/kh/ph/ṛh/th/ṭh** = *breathed*. **ḍ/ṛ/ṭ** = *flapped*.

Urdu Dictionary & Phrasebook · 33

K/KH

kā of
kab? when?
kabab kebab
kabhī-kabhī sometimes
kabhī nahīṅ never
kābīna cabinet *political*
kaccā raw
kacrā garbage; litter
kaddū pumpkin
kāfī enough; sufficient; **kāfi vaqt se** for a long time; **Kāfī hai!** That's enough!
kāğaz paper; **kāğaz kā tukṛā** a piece of paper
kahāṅ? where?; **kahaṅ hai?** where is?; **kahāṅ haiṅ?** where are?; **kahāṅ se?** where from?
kahānī story
kahāvat proverb
kāhil lazy
kahīṅ bhī anywhere
kahīṅ nahīṅ nowhere
kahīṅ per somewhere
ka'ī many; several
kaimre kī film film for camera
kaise how
kājal mascara
kakṛī melon
kal tomorrow; yesterday
kālā black; **kālā bāzār** black market
kalā'ī wrist
kalejā liver
kalī mirc pepper
kam short; less
kām job; performance; work; **kām kar** to work; **kām karne vālā** worker
kamā'ī earnings
kamar back; **kamar meiṅ dard** backache
kambal blanket
kamī shortage; lack
kamrā room
kamre kā nambar room number
kamre kī "service" room service
kāmyābī success
kamzor weak
kān ear
kanastar canister
kandhā shoulder
kaṅg-ghā comb
kapās cotton
kāpī (photo)copy; **kāpī kar** to (photo)copy
kāpī notebook
kapṛe clothes; **kapṛe dhone kā pauḍar** washing powder; **kapṛe kī dukān** clothes shop; **kapṛe laṭkāne kā haiṅgar** clothes hanger; **kapṛe pehaṅye** to put on clothes
kar to do; **kar saknā** to be able
kaṛā bracelet
kār-āmad useful
kār-kun activist
kaṛvā sour
kārxāna factory
kashtī boat; ferry
kasrat exercise
kasṭam kī "duty" customs duty
kāṭ to cut; to chop; to bite
kāṭa fork
kāṭnā amputation
kaun who; **kaun sā?** which?
kā'ūnṭar counter; booth
kavā crow
ke that *preposition*
keh to say; to tell
ketlī kettle
khā eat
khād fertilizer
khadān mine *mineral*
khā'ī ravine

khail-kūd sports; athletics
khaiṅc to pull
khāna food; meal
khanḍar ruins
khāne meals; **khāne kā āḍar de** to order a meal; **khāne kā kamrā** dining room; **khāne kā tel** cooking oil
khaṛā ho to stand
khāṛī bay; **khaṛī kar** to park
khaṛo flock
khaṭ-khaṭā to knock
khel game; show; play
khetī-bāṛī farming; agriculture
khilā to feed
khilāṛī sportsman; athlete
khiṛkī booth; window
khod to dig
khoj exploration
khol to open; to switch on
khujlī itch
khulā open; clear
kīcaṛ mud
kilo kilogram
kilomiter kilometer
kināra shore
kīṛā insect; fly
kirā'e per le to hire
kirāya fare; freight
kīṛe insects; **kīṛe mārne kī davā** insecticide
kis taraf? which direction?
kis tarah kā? what kind of?
kisān farmer
kisī tarah se somehow
kitāb book
kitāb ghar bookshop
kitnā? how much?
kitne (sāre)? how many?
kiyā? what?; **Kiyā vaqt hai?** What time is it?; **Kiyā mushkil hai?** What's the trouble?
kiyoṅ? why?
koelā coal; **koele kā ingin** locomotive; **koele kī khadān** coal mine
ko'ī someone; somebody; **ko'ī cīz** something; **ko'ī bhī** anyone; **ko'ī nahīṅ** nobody; **ko'ī bhī nahīṅ** neither; **Ko'ī bāt nahīṅ hai.** It doesn't matter.
kork kholne kī cābī corkscrew
koshish kar to try
kuch some; **kuch nahīṅ** nothing
kūd to leap
kudāl spade; pickax
kuhar fog; **kuhar ālūd** foggy
kuhnī elbow
kursī chair
kushṭī wrestling
kuttā dog
kūvaṅ well *noun*

L

lā to get; to bring
lagā to plant; to grow
lag-bhag approximately; more or less
lā'īq worthy
lakṛī wood; stick; **lakṛī kā pālish** varnish
lālī pāp candy
lambā long; tall
lambā'ī length
lambī ser to hike
lamhā moment
lapeṭ to wrap
laṛ to fight
lāṛī truck
laṛkā boy; son
laṛkī girl; daughter
laṛne vāla fighter
latīfā joke
laṭkā to hang

lazīz tasty
le to take
lehāf duvet
lekin but
leṭ jā to lie down
libās dress *noun*
lifā-fā envelope
lift elevator
likh to write
likhā'ī writing
likhne kā kāğaz writing paper
līmū lemon
līp kā sāl leap year
līvar lever
log people
luğat dictionary
lūṭ to rob

M

ma'āshirat society
ma'āshiratī social
ma'āshiyāt economics
ma'āvizā compensation
ma'danīyāt minerals
mā'danī-yātī pānī mineral water
Ma'ī May
ma'īshat economy *of country*
machchar dānī mosquito net
machchar mosquito
machlī fish; **machlī pakaṛnā** fishing; **maclī pakaṛne kā jāl** fishing net
māda female
madad help; **madad kar** to help
madrasā madrasa
māf karna! sorry! *familiar*
māf kaṛye! sorry! *formal*
māfī apology
mağrib west
mağribī west(ern)
mağrūr proud
mahfūz jagā shelter
mahīna month
māhir consultant; expert
māhir-e-lisāniyāt linguist
miahir-e-ma'āshiyāt economist
māhvārī period; menstruation
maidān field
maile kapṛe laundry
maiṅ I; me; **maiṅ xud** myself
makṛī spider
maktab school
māl material
mālī financial
mālik owner
malūmāt information; knowledge
malūmātī daftar information office
māṅ mother
manā forbidden; **manā kar** to forbid
mandir temple
maṅgal Tuesday
manshiyāt drug; narcotics; **manshiyāt kā nāshā karne vāla** drug addict
mansūx cancel
manzār view
manzil floor; story
maqsad goal *aim*
mar to die
mār to hit; to beat; to kill
marā dead
Mārc March
marham-paṭṭī band-aid
marīz patient *medical*
markaz center; base; headquarters
mashhūr well-known
māshīn machine
mashriq east *noun*
mashriqī east(ern) *adjective*
masjid mosque
maslā problem

maslāla dār spicy; hot
masnū'ī artificial
masrūf busy
masūm innocent
masūṛā gum(s) *of mouth*
mat not
"match" match *sports*
matlab meaning
mau'jūd remain
mauj (sea) wave
maujūdā contemporary
mausam climate; weather; season
maut death
mauzūṅ suitable
mavāzinā comparison; **mavāzinā kar** to compare
maveshī cattle
mazā pleasure; taste
mazāq humor; joke; **mazāq kar** to joke
mazāqī funny; humorous
mazār tomb
mazbūt strong
maze-dār enjoyable; tasty
maz-hab religion
māzī kā past *adjective*
mazlūm victim
mazmūn essay; subject
mehal palace
mehfūz safe
mehmān guest; visitor
mehrūm deprived; **mehrūm kar** to deprive
mehsūs kar to feel
meiṅ in; into; among
meṅḍak frog
meṅhgā expensive
menu menu
merā my
"meter" meter *measure*
mez table
mezbān host
mīl mile
milā to add; to receive; to shake; to dissolve
mill to meet
minārā minaret
mircī vāla spicy; hot
mirgī epilepsy
misāl example
mīṭhā sweet
miṭhā'ī desserts; sweet(s); candy
mo'arix historian
model model
modem modem
modern modern
mohur stamp *official*
mojizā miracle
mom-battī candlestick
moṛ corner; bend
moṭā fat; thick
motī pearl
mozā sock
mu'āhidā contract
mudīr editor
muft free *of charge*
muhabbat love
Muhtarimā Ms
mujasamā statue
mujrim criminal
mulāqāt meeting
mulāzimīn staff; employees
mulk country; nation; state
mulkī national
mumkin possible; probable; **mumkin hai** to be likely
mūṅ mouth
munazim administrator
mūṅch moustache
muntaqil kar/de to transmit
muntaxib kar to elect
muqāblā competition; contest
muqaddamā trial *legal*
muqarir mehmān guest speaker
muqarir speaker

c = *church.* **ṅ** = *sing.* **x** = *loch.* **ğ/q** *see p18.* **bh/ch/dh/ḍh/gh/kh/ph/ṛh/th/ṭh** = *breathed.* **ḍ/ṛ/ṭ** = *flapped.*

muṛ to turn
murāsilāt communications
murğī chicken; hen
musāfir passenger; traveler
Musalmān Muslim
musanif author; writer
musavidā document
musavir photographer
musavirī photography
mushkil difficult
mūsīqī music
musnū'ī hāth-pair artificial limb
mustaqbil future
mutābiq: ke mutābiq according to
mutma'in satisfied
muxālifat opposition
muxtasar short
muzāfāt suburb

N

nā not; **nā jā'iz** illegal; **nā mumkin** impossible; **nā xush** unhappy
nā'ī barber; hairdresser
nā'ib sadar vice-president
nā'o ferry
nāc dance; to dance
nadī river; **nadī kā kināra** river bank
nafrat hatred; **nafrat kar** to hate
nahā to bathe
nahīṅ no; not
nākāmī failure
nālī gun barrel
nalkī tube
nām name; noun; **Merā nām Emma hai.** My name is Emma.
namak salt
namāz prayers
namkīn salty
nāṅk nose
nāp size
nāp-tol to measure
naqal copy
naqsh inscription
naqshā map; **Pākistān kā naqsha** map of Pakistan
nar male
naram soft
narangī orange *color*
nārāz annoyed; **nārāz honā** to be annoyed
narm polite
nāshist seat; session
nāshtā breakfast
nau nine
naukrī job
nauxaiz infant
navve ninety
nāxun nail; **nāxun kāṭne kī mashīn** nail-clippers
nayā new; **nayā cānd** new moon
nazam poem
nazar sight; **nazar rakh** to watch
nazāra view
nazm system
neher canal
nībū lemon; lime; **nībū kī cā'e** tea with lemon
nīcā low
nīce below; down; under
nigal to swallow
nikāl to exit; to withdraw
nikalne kā rāsta exit
nīlā blue
nīṅd āna to feel sleepy
nīnd kī golī sleeping pills
nishān mark; sign; symbol
no'īyat significance
novel novel *noun§*
numā'inda representative

numā'indagī representation; **numā'indagī kar** to represent
numā'ish exhibition; **numā'ish kar** to exhibit
nuqsān loss
Nuvember November

O

o and

P/PH

pa'hāṛ mountain
pā'oṅ foot
pacās fifty
pādrī priest
pāgal insane; **pāgal kutte ke kāṭne kī bīmārī** rabies
pāgal-pan insanity
pagḍanḍī track; path
pahāṛ hill; mountain; **pahaṛ kī cotī** mountain peak; **pahaṛī ilāqa** mountain range
paidā kar to yield; to give birth
paidā'ish birth; **paidāish kī jagā** place of birth; **paidāishī "certificate"** birth certificate
paida-vār yield
paiğām message
paisā money; **paisā bacā** to save money
pakā ripe; to cook
pakaṛ to hold
Pākistān Pakistan
Pākistānī Pakistani
palag plug
pānā spanner
pāna wrench *tool*
paṅc five
pandrā fifteen
pāne tools
pānī water; **panī kā "glass"** glass of water; **panī kī botal** bottle of water; **pīne kā pānī** drinking water; **Panī kī lā'in kaṭ ga'ī hai.** The water has been cut off.; **panī kā jahāz** ship
panīr cheese
paṅkhā fan
pants trousers
pā'oṅ kā paṅja toe
pār through; **pār kar** to cross
paraishān worried; **paraishān ho** to worry
paraishānī trouble; worry
parcā magazine
paṛh to read; to study
paṛhā to teach
paṛhā'ī reading; study
paṛosī neighbor
Pārsī Zoroastrian
parsoṅ the day before yesterday; the day after tomorrow
party party
pas pass *noun*
pās kī local; **pās kī dūkān** local shop
pasand kar to like
patā address
paṭā belt
patā calā/kar to find out; to discover
path-thar stone
patlā thin
patlūn trousers
pattā leaf
patta-gobhī lettuce
paudā plant; **paudā lagānā** planting
pāuḍar powder
pāxāna toilet
payām message

pehan to wear
pehcān identification; to recognize
pehilvānī wrestling
pehlā first; **pehlā darjā** first class
pehle before; previously
peṅc-kash screwdriver
per on; onto
peshā occupation; profession
peshavar professional
peṭ stomach; **peṭ kā dard** stomach ache
petrol petrol
peyālī cup
phailā spread
phaipṛe lungs
phal fruit; **phal kā bāğ** orchard; **phal kā ras** fruit juice; **phal pānā** reaping
phallī beans
phā'oṛā shovel
phāṛ to tear
phaṭā to burst; to explode
pheṅk to throw
phir again; then; **phir bhī** still *adverb*; **phir se kar** to repeat
phisal to slip
phoṅk to blow
phoṛā boil; ulcer
phūl flower; **phūl vāla/phūl valī** florist
phuvār drizzle; **Phuvār paṛ rahī hai.** It's drizzling.
pī to drink
piano piano
pīche backwards; behind; **pichle hafte** last week; **pichle sāl** last year
pīlā yellow
pin pin
Pīr Monday
pīs to grind
pistaul pistol
piyār love; **piyār kar** to love
piyāre dear; loved
piyāsa thirsty
plāstar plaster; splint
plastik plastic
platform platform
polo polo
post post; mail; **post se** by post
postkāṛd postcard
potā grandson
potī granddaughter
"pound" pound
pūch to ask
pūch-tāch enquiry
pukār to cry; to weep
pul bridge
pūrā full; whole; entire; **pūrā cānd** full moon
purānā old; senior; past; second-hand
purānā daur past *noun*
puranī dushmanī feud
purkhe ancestors
purse wallet

Q

qabar grave
qābiz fauj occupying forces
qabrastān cemetery
qābū control
qabz constipation; occupation *of a country*
qadīm ancient
qaid prison
qā'id leader
qaidī prisoner
qā'im kar to establish
qaiṅcī scissors
qalam pen
qalb heart
qālīn carpet

a = apple. **ā** = father. **e** = pay. **i** = sit. **ī** = heat. **o** = hotel. **u** = put. **ū** = shoot. **au** = oar. **ai** = pay.

qamīs shirt
qānūn law
qānūnī legal
qarār-dāt agreement
qaraz le to borrow
qarīb near; **qarīb meiṅ** nearby
qarīb-qarīb almost
qarz debt; credit; **qarz per** on credit ; **qarz de** to lend
qasā'ī butcher
qatal murder; killing; **qatal kar** to kill; to murder
qatār row; line
qātil murderer; killer
qatl-e-ām genocide
qaum community
qavā'id grammar
qāzī judge
qe to vomit
qilā fort
qilat shortage
qīmat cost; price; rate
qism kind; type
qismat luck
qiyādat kar to lead
qiyādat leadership
qos-e-qazah rainbow
qudrat nature
qudratī natural; **qudratī zarā'e** natural resources
Qurān Quran
qutub numā compass
qūvat strength

R

rad-e-amal reaction
"radio" radio; **"radio" kā program** radio program; **"radio" nashriyāt** radio broadcast
raftār speed
rag artery; vein
rā'ī mustard
rail gaṛī train
raiṛh kī haḍḍī spine
rāj dhāni capital city
rakābī plate
rakh to put; to keep; to store
Ramzān Ramadan
rang color; **rang kar** to paint
rānī queen
raqam amount; payment
rasī rope; string; **"tow" karne kī rasī** tow rope
rasīd receipt
rāstā path; route; access
rāste kī rukāvaṭ roadblock
rāt night; **rāt kā caukidār** night guard; night watchman
raushnī light *not dark*
raza'ī duvet; quilt
registān desert
reh to dwell
rehim-dil kind
rehne kī jagā accommodation
rehnumā'ī kar to guide
rel gaṛī kā isṭeshan train station
resham silk
ret sand
rikauḍ kar to record
rishte dār relatives
rivāj custom; tradition
rivāyat tradition
rivāyatī folk; traditional
rivāyatī bāteṅ folklore
rivāyatī mosīqī folk music
rivāyatī nāc folk dancing
riyāsat state *in federation*
Riyāsat-e-Muttahida-e-Amarīkā United States of America
ro to weep
rok to stop *someone;* **rok thām kar** to contain
rotī bread

c = *church.* **ṅ** = *sing.* **x** = *loch.* **ğ/q** *see p18.* **bh/ch/dh/ḍh/gh/kh/ph/ṛh/th/ṭh** = *breathed.* **ḍ/ṛ/ṭ** = *flapped.*

rozī wages
rūh soul
rū'ī cotton
ruk to stop; **rukye!** stop!
Rūs Russia
Rūsī Russian

S/SH

sab all; **sab sāth** all together
sabab reason; cause
sabaq chapter; lesson
sabar patience; **sabar kar** to be patient
sābit kar to prove
sābun soap
sabzī vegetables; **sabzī kī dūkān** vegetable shop; **sabzī vāla** greengrocer; **sabzī xor** vegetarian
sac true
saccā'ī truth
sāda plain *noun*
sadar president; head of state; **sadar kā "guard"** presidential guard
sadī century
sadmā trauma
sadrī jacket
sāf clean; clear; **sāf kar** to clean
safā'ī hygiene
safaid white
safar travel; **safār kā "timetable"** travel timetable; **safar karne kī vajeh** reason for travel; **safar kar** to travel
safīr ambassador
sahāfī journalist
sahī correct; right; **sahī kar** to correct
sā'ikal bicycle
sailāb flood
sā'ins science
sā'ins dāṅ scientist
sā'insī scientific
sa'īyāh tourist
sāl year
salād salad
salāh truce
salām alekum! hello!; *response:* **vālekum salām!**
sāl-girā birthday
samāj society
samajh sense; **samajh dārī** wisdom
samajhā to understand; to realize; **Āp samajhte haiṅ?** Do you understand?
samājī social
sāmān baggage; equipment; **sāmān kī khiṛkī** baggage counter
samandar sea; **samandar kā kināra** beach; shore; **samandar ke qarīb** coast
sāmne opposite
sānḍ bull; ax
Sanīcar Saturday
sānihā disaster
sāṅolā brown
sāṅp snake; **sāṅp kā kāṭā** snake bite
sāṅs breath
santarā orange *fruit*
sar head; **sar dard** headache
saṛak road; street; **saṛak kā naqshā** road map
sardār head; boss; chief
sardī cold; **sardī kā mausam** winter
sarhad border; frontier; **sarhad pār jānā** border crossing
sarhadī caukī-dār border guard
sastā cheap
sāt seven
satah level

a = apple. **ā** = father. **e** = pay. **i** = sit. **ī** = heat. **o** = hotel. **u** = put. **ū** = shoot. **au** = oar. **ai** = pay.

sāth together; with
sāṭh sixty
sāthī colleague; companion
satrā seventeen
sattar seventy
sau hundred
savāl question
savāneh-umri biography
saxt hard; firm
sāyā shade
sazā de to punish
"school" school
se than
se achchā better
seb apple
sehat health; **sehat mand** healthy
seṅk to bake; to heat
seṅkā hūvā baked; heated
shab baxair! good night!
shabnam mist
shādī marriage
shadīd severe; **shadīd garmī** severe heat; **shadīd sard** freezing
shafā cure; healing
shāgird pupil
shāhī royal
shahīd martyr
shāh-kār legend
shāh-rāh highway; motorway
shā'id maybe; perhaps
shaihid honey
shaimpū shampoo
shā'ir poet
shaitān devil
shak doubt
shakar sugar
shakar ki bimārī diabetes
shām evening; p.m.; **shām kā khāna** dinner; supper
shamā candle
shāmil included
shāmil ho to participate
shamīyāna tent
shanaxtī kārd I.D. card
shāndār splendid
sharāb alcoholic drink; wine; **sharāb kā nashā karnā** to get drunk
sharbat drink
shatranj chess
shauhar husband
shaxs person
shehar town; city; **shehar kā corāha** town square; **shehar kā "hall"** city hall; **shehar kā markaz** town center; **shehar ke bare meiṅ** about town; **shehar kā naqshā** city map
shehid kī makh-khī bee
shehrī citizen; civilian
shehrī huqūq civil rights
shehrīyat nationality; citizenship
shikār kā ilāqa game reserve
shikāyat complaint
shīshā glass
shok shock *medical*
shor-o-ğul noise
shumāl north
shumālī north(ern)
Shumālī "Ireland" Northern Ireland
shurū kar to begin
shurū'āt beginning
sī to sew
sīdhā right; straight
sīdhe straight on; **Sīdhe jā'īye.** Go straight ahead.
sifar zero; nought
sifārat xānā embassy; consulate
sifāratī ta'aluqāt diplomatic ties
sigareṭ pīnā smoking
sīkh to learn

c = *church.* **ṅ** = *sing.* **x** = *loch.* **ğ/q** *see p18.* **bh/ch/dh/ḍh/gh/kh/ph/ṛh/th/ṭh** = *breathed.* **ḍ/ṛ/ṭ** = *flapped.*

sikkā coin; **sikkā rā'ij-ul-vaqt** currency
sikke coins
simt direction
sīnā chest; breast
sīne kī mashīn sewing machine
sipāhī troops
sīpī shell
sirf only
sīṛhī ladder
sirkā vinegar
Sitambar September
sitāra star
siyāhat tourism
siyāhī ink
siyāsat politics; **siyāsat dāṅ** politician
siyāsī political; **siyasī "party"** political party
so to sleep
sola sixteen
sonā gold
soṅc to think
sone kā beg sleeping bag
sone kā kamrā bedroom
sone kā zevar gold jewelry
"station" station
subah morning; a.m.
subah-subah dawn
subūt proof; evidence
sūd interest *financial*
suhbat sex
sū'ī needle
sun to hear; to listen
supurd kar to hand over
sūraj sun; **sūraj ḍhalnā** sunset
suraṅg tunnel
sūrāx hole; **sūrāx kar** to drill a hole
surx red
sust lazy
sūtī kapṛā cotton cloth
sūvar pig; **sūvar kā gosht** pork

T/Ṭ/TH/ṬH

ta'ajub xez surprising
ta'aluq connection; relationship
ta'aruf introduction; **ta'aruf kar** to introduce
ta'āvun cooperation
ṭab bath
tab: tab bhī still *adverb*; **tab se** since
tabdīl kar to replace; to change; to exchange; **Āp paisā tabdīl karte haiṅ?** Do you exchange money?
tabsirā review
taftīsh investigation; **taftīsh kar** to investigate
ṭā'ī necktie
taiks tax
tair to float; to swim
tairnā swimming; **tairne kā pūl** swimming pool; **tairne ke kapṛe** swimsuit
taiz spicy; hot
tājir businessman
tajziyā analysis
ṭāke surgical stitches
ṭakkar to crash
taklīf pain; symptom
taklīf-de uncomfortable
taknīk technique
taknīkī technical
taksī taxi
takyā pillow
tālā lock; **tālā lagā** to lock
talafuz accent; pronunciation
talāq divorce
talāsh hunt; exploration
talāsh kar to find; to seek
talib-e-ilm student
tālīm education
talx bitter
tamancā pistol

a = apple. **ā** = father. **e** = pay. **i** = sit. **ī** = heat. **o** = hotel. **u** = put. **ū** = shoot. **au** = oar. **ai** = pay.

ṭamāṭar tomato
tāmbā copper
tambākū tobacco; **tambākū noshī manā hai** no smoking
tambū tent
tamīz dār polite
tanāsulī genitals
taṅg narrow
ṭāṅg leg
tank tank
tanxā pay
tāqat power
taqrīb party
taqrīban approximately; nearly; more or less
taqsīm divide
tār wire; telex
taraf direction
tarah kind; type
taraqī development
tarbūz melon; watermelon
tārīf kar to praise
tārīk dark *adjective*
tarīqā way; system
tārīx date; history
tarīx-e-paidā'ish date of birth
tarjumā translation; interpretation
tarjumā kar to translate; to interpret
tarjumān translator; interpreter
tarkīb syntax
tasbīh rosary
tashaddud violence
tashxīs diagnosis
tasvīr picture; photo
tauhfā present; gift
tauliyā towel
taxt throne
tayārī preparation
tayār kar to prepare
tayār-shuda māl product
tāza fresh
tehat: ke tehat under
tehqīq research
tehvār festival
teh xānā cellar
tehzīb culture
tel oil; **tel kā cirāğ** fuel dump; **tel kā ḍabba** oilcan; **tel kā kūvaṅ** oil well
ṭelīvizhan television
"tennis" tennis
terā thirteen
teyār ready
tez sharp; **tezī se** fast; **tez raftār** express
thailā sack
thailī carrier bag
thakā tired
thakāne vāla tiring
thakāvaṭ tiredness
thānā police station
ṭhanḍā cold; cool; **ṭhanḍā panī** cold water
ṭhīk normal; suitable; **ṭhīk kar** to improve; to repair
ṭhīk karnā repair
ṭhiṅgnā short *height*
thoṛā little; **thoṛā sā** a little bit
thuḍḍī chin
thūk to spit
tibbī medical; **tibbī imdād** first aid
tijārat business
tijārtī kām business work
tijārtī log business class
ṭīkā lagā to vaccinate; **ṭīkā lagā hūvā** vaccinated
ṭikiṭ ticket
ṭikiṭ ghar ticket office
tīm team
tīn three; **tīn dafā** three times; thrice; **tīn cauthā'ī** three-quarters
tīs thirty

tīsrā third *adjective*
titlī butterfly
tohfā gift
ṭolī group
ṭoṅtī faucet; tap
top cannon; gun
toṛ to break
tūfān storm
tūfanī olā-bārī blizzard
tulū āftāb sunrise
Turkī Turk; Turkish; Turkey

U/Ū

ubāl to boil
udās sad
ugā grow *crops*
ujāla light *not dark*
uljhan confusion
ullū owl
umar age; **Āp kī umar kiyā hai?** How old are you?; **Merī umar ... sāl hai.** I am ... years old.
umīd kar expect
ūn wool
ūncā high
unglī finger; **unglī kā nāxun** fingernail
unkā their
unke them
unnīs nineteen
ūṅṭ camel
ūpar top; up
uqāb eagle
uṛā to fly; to blow up
uṛān flight; **uṛān bhar** take off
us him; her; it; **us kā** his; her; its; **us ke jaisā** like that; **us ke sāmne** in front of; **us taraf** that way; **us vajeh se** for that reason
ustād teacher
utār slope
uṭh to rise; to wake up
uṭhā to lift; to raise

V

vabā epidemic
vādī valley
vafd member
vahaṅ there; **Vahaṅ pānī hai?** Is there any water?; **Vahāṅ per hadisā hūvā hai.** There has been an accident.
vā'in vine
vājbī must; have to
vajeh reason
vakīl lawyer
valī saint
vālidain parents
van van
vāpasī return; **vāpasī kā ṭikiṭ** return ticket
vaqfā break; interval
vaqt time; period; moment; **vaqt per** on time
vatan homeland
vazāhat explanation
vazan weight
vāzih kar to explain
vazīr minister
vazir-e-āzam prime minister
vazrāt ministry; **Vazrāt-e-Difā** Ministry of Defense; **Vazrāt-e-Insāf/Adal** Ministry of Justice; **Vazrāt-e-Sehat** Ministry of Health; **Vazrāt-e-Tālīm** Ministry of Education; **Vazrāt-e-Xārja** Ministry of Foreign Affairs; **Vazrāt-e-Zirā'at** Ministry of Agriculture
"virus" virus

a = apple. **ā** = father. **e** = pay. **i** = sit. **ī** = heat. **o** = hotel. **u** = put. **ū** = shoot. **au** = oar. **ai** = pay.

viza visa
vo he; she; it; they; that; those
vo xud himself; herself; itself; themselves
vot vote; **vot de** to vote

X

xāb dream
xabar news
xaccar pony; mule
xāhish wish; **xāhish kar** to want
xairātī charity; **xairātī tanzīm** charity organization
xalā space
xālī empty; free
xalī kar to empty; to drain
xāmūsh silent
xāmūshī silence; **xāmūshī se** silently
xāna drawer
xānā-jangī civil war
xāndān family
xāndānī mansūbā-bandī birth control
xandānī nām surname
xarāb serious; grave; **xarāb galā** sore throat
xarāsh bruise
xarbūz melon; watermelon
xarc kar spend
xardār tār barbed wire
xargosh rabbit
xarīd to buy
xarīdārī shopping
xās tor per especially
xat letter
xatam end
xātam kar to end; to destroy
xatrā danger; risk
xatrā le to risk
xauf fear; **xauf zadā** afraid
xāvind husband
xhūn murder *verb*
xilāl toothpick
xinzīr pig
xiyāl idea; thought
xof zadā to frighten
xūb sūrat beautiful
xūb sūrtī beauty
xud kā own
xud muxtār autonomous; independent
xud muxtārī autonomy; independence
Xudā God
xudā hāfiz! good-bye!
xufyā secret; **xufyā police** secret police
xūn blood; killing; murder; **xūn denā** blood transfusion; **xūn kā grūp** blood group; **xūn jamnā** thrombosis; **Xūn beh rahā hai.** It is bleeding.
xush happy
xush āmded! welcome!

Y

yā or
yād kar to remember
yāddāsht memory
yādgār monument; souvenir
yahāṅ here
Yahūdī Jew; Jewish
Yahūdīyat Judaism
yaqīnī certain
yaqīnī taur per certainly
yatīm orphan
yatīm xāna orphanage
ye this; these
Yūnān Greece
Yūnānī Greek

c = *church.* **ṅ** = *sing.* **x** = *loch.* **ğ/q** *see p18.* **bh/ch/dh/ḍh/gh/kh/ph/ṛh/th/ṭh** = *breathed.* **ḍ/ṛ/ṭ** = *flapped.*

Z

zabān language; tongue
zaihar poison
zālim cruel
zalzalā earthquake
zamīn land; earth; ground; **zamīn doz** underground; **zamīn kā khisaknā** landslide
zanā bil jabar rape
zang rust
zanjīr chain; **zanjīr kā tālā** padlock
zarā'at agriculture
zara-e-haml-o-naqal transport
zarā sā too little
Zartash Zoroastrian
zarūrat need
zarūrī have to; must
zarxez fertile
zaryā source
zaxam injury; wound; bruise
zaxmī injured; **zaxmī hūnā** to be injured; **zaxmī kar** to injure
zevar jewelry
zilā district
zindā alive
zindagī life
zīrāks kāpī photocopy
zīrāks kī mashīn photocopier
ziyāda more; much; extra; excess; **sab se ziyāda** most; **ziyāda nahīṅ** not much; **ziyāda sāmān** excess baggage; **ziyāda pasand kar** to prefer
zor pressure; **zor kī āvāz** loud; **zor se** loudly; **zor lagā** to press
zukām cold *medical*

ENGLISH–URDU ANGREZĪ–URDŪ

A

able: to be able kar saknā
about: I'll see about it. Maiṅ us ke bare meiṅ āp se milūṅgā.; **about 50 miles** lag bhag pacās mīl; **about town** shehar ke bare meiṅ
academy "academy"
accelerator "accelerator"
accent talafuz
access rāstā; **Do you have access for the disabled?** Āp ke pās apāhij logoṅ ke lī'ye intizām hai?
accident hādisā; **There has been an accident.** Vahāṅ per hadisā hūvā hai.
accommodation rehne kī jagā
according to ke mutābiq
account *financial* hisāb
accuse ilzām lagā
activist kār-kun
actor adā-kār
actual asal
adapter *electric* bijlī kā "adapter"
add *verb* milā
addition: in addition to this is ke alāva
address patā
administrator munazim
adventure "adventure"
advert ishtihār
afraid *adjective* xauf zadā
after bād; **after supper** khāne ke bād; **one after another** ek ke bād ek
afternoon dopehar
this afternoon āj shām ko
afterwards ke bād
again phir
age umar
ago: long ago bohut pehle; **a year ago** ek sāl pehle
agreement qarār-dāt
agriculture zarā'at; khetī-bāṛī
agronomist "agronomist"
aid imdād; **first aid** tibbī imdād
AIDS "AIDS"
air havā
air conditioner "aircondition"
airfield havā'ī maidān
air force havā'ī fauj
airline "airline"
air mail havā'ī ḍāk
airplane havā'ī jahāz
airport hava'ī aḍḍā
airport tax "airport tax"; havā'ī aḍḍāy kā ṭaiks
alcohol "alcohol"
alcoholic drink sharāb
alive *adjective* zindā
all sab; **all together** sab sāth
allergic: I'm allergic to antibiotics Mujhe antibiotics se "allergy" hai.
allergy "allergy"
allow *noun* ijāzat
almost qarīb-qarīb

c = *church.* **ṅ** = *sing.* **x** = *loch.* **ğ/q** *see p18.* **bh/ch/dh/ḍh/gh/kh/ph/ṛh/th/ṭh** = *breathed.* **ḍ/ṛ/ṭ** = *flapped.*

Urdu Dictionary & Phrasebook · 49

alone akele
alphabet hurūf
also bhī
alter badal
although hālāṅ ke
altitude sickness "altitude sickness"
always hameṅshā'
a.m. subah
ambassador safīr
ambulance "ambulance"
America "America"
American Amrīkī
among meiṅ
amount raqam
amputation kāṭnā
analysis tajziyā
ancestors ābā-o-ajdād; purkhe
ancient qadīm
and aur
anesthetic be-hoshī kī davā; "anesthetic"
anesthetist "anesthetist"
anger ğusā
angle farishtā
angry *adjective* ğusā; **to be angry** ğusā kar
animal jānvar
ankle taxnā
annoyed nārāz; **to be annoyed** nārāz ho
another dūsrā; **another bottle** dūsrī botal
answer *noun* javāb; *verb* javāb de
ant cūṅṭī
antibiotic "antibiotic"
anti-freeze "anti-freeze"
antiseptic "antiseptic"
anyone ko'ī bhī
anywhere kahīṅ bhī
apartment "apartment"
apartment block "apartment" vālī bilḍing
apologize: I apologize. Maiṅ māfī maṅgtā hūṅ.
apology māfī
appear *verb* nazar ā
apple seb
appliances ālāt
approximately taqrīban; lag-bhag
April Aprel
Arab Arab
Arabic *language* Arabī zabān
archeology āsār-e-qadīma
architect "architect"
architecture "architecture"
area ilāqā
arm bāzū
armored car "armored" gaṛī
arms *weapons* hathyār
army fauj
arrange intizām
arrest giraftār
arrive āyā
artery rag
art gallery "art gallery"
artificial masnū'ī
artificial limb musnū'ī hāth-pair
artillery "artillery"
artist fan kār
arts funon
ashtray "ashtray"
ask *verb* pūch
aspirin "aspirin"
assassin qātil
assassination qatal; xūn
asthma damma
athlete khilaṛī
athletics khail-kūd
atlas atlas
attack *noun* hamlā; *verb* hamlā kar
aunt *see page 98.*
Australia "Australia"

Australian Austrailia'ī
author musanif
autonomous xud muxtār
autonomy xud muxtārī
average *adjective* darmiyāna; ām
awake: to be awake jāg
ax bail; sānḍ

B

baby baccā
back *noun* kamar
backache kamar meiṅ dard
backpack "backpack"
backwards pīche
bacteria "bacteria"
bad burā
badly burī tareh se
bag beg
baggage sāmān; **excess baggage** ziyāda sāmān
baggage counter sāmān kī khiṛkī
bake *verb* seṅk
baked seṅkā hūvā
bakery "bakery"
balcony "balcony"
ball gend
band-aid marham-paṭṭī
bandit ḍākū
bank bank; *of river* nadī kā kināra
banker "banker"
banknotes bank ke "notes"
banquet baṛī dāvat
bar "bar"
barbed wire xār-dār tār
barber hajām; nā'ī
barley jo
barn bāṛa
barracks "barracks"
barrel ḍaram; *gun* nālī
barren uājṛ
bartender bār vāla
base markaz
basin "basin"
basis bunyād
basket "basket"
basketball "basketball"
bath ṭab
bathe nahā
bathroom ğusal-xānā
battery "battery"
battle jaṅg
bay khāṛī
be honā
beach samandar kā kināra
beans phallī
beard dāṛhī
beat mār
beautiful xūb sūrat
beauty xūb sūrtī
beauty parlor "beauty parlor"
because of kī vajeh se
become ban
bed bistar; **to go to bed** so
bedroom sone kā kamrā
bee shehid kī makh-khī
beef gā'e kā gosht
beer "beer"
before pehle
begin shurū kar
beginning shurū'āt
behind pīche
believe yaqīn
bell ghanṭī
below nīce
belt paṭā; "belt"
bend *noun: in road* moṛ; *verb* jhuk
besides *preposition* ke alāva
best sab se achchanote
better se achchā
between darmiyān
bicycle sā'ikal

c = *church*. ṅ = *sing*. x = *loch*. ğ/q *see p18*. bh/ch/dh/ḍh/gh/kh/ph/ṛh/th/ṭh = *breathed*. ḍ/ṛ/ṭ = *flapped*.

big baṛā
biggest sab se baṛā
bill "bill"
binoculars dūr-bīn
biography savāneh-umri
bird cuṛyā
birth *noun* paidā'ish; **to give birth** bacca de; jannā
birth certificate paidāishī "certificate"
birth control xāndānī mansūbā-bandī
birthday sāl-girā
bit hisā; **a little bit** thoṛā
bite *verb* kāṭ
bitter talx
black kālā
black market kālā bazār
blanket kambal
bleed: It is bleeding. Xūn beh rahā hai.
blind andhā
blizzard tūfanī olā-bārī
blocked band
blood xūn
blood group xūn kā grūp
blood pressure "blood pressure"
blood transfusion xūn denā; "blood transfusion"
blow *verb* phoṅk
blow up *explode* uṛā
blue nīlā
boarding pass "boarding pass"
boat kashtī
body jism
boil *noun* phoṛā; *verb* bāl
bomb bam
bombardment bam-bārī
bone haḍḍī
bonnet *of car* "car" kā bāneṭ
booby trap "booby trap"
book *noun* kitāb
bookshop kitāb ghar
boot *of car* ḍikkī
booth khiṛkī; **cashier's booth** "cashier" kī khiṛkī
boots baṛe jūte
border sarhad
border crossing sarhad pār jānā
border guard sarhadī caukī-dār
borrow qaraz le
boss baṛā sāhib; "boss"
both donoṅ
bottle botal; **bottle of water** panī kī botal
bottle-opener botal kholne kī cābī
bottom niche
box ḍabba
boxing ghoṅsā bāzī
boy laṛkā
boyfriend "boyfriend"
bracelet kaṛā
brake "brake"
brave bahadur
bread roṭī
break *noun: from work* vaqfā; *verb* toṛ
break down: Our car has broken down. Hamarī gaṛī xarāb ho ga'ī hai.
breakfast nāshtā
breast sīna
breath sāṅs
brick īṅṭ
bridge pul
bring lā
Britain Bartāniyā
British *person* Angrez; *thing* Angrezī
brother bhā'ī
brown sāṅolā
bruise xarāsh; zaxam
brush brash
bucket bālṭī
budget "budget"

build banā
building imārat
bull sāṅḍ
bullet golī
bumper "bumper"
bureaucracy "bureaucracy"
burn *verb* jalā
burst *verb* phaṭā; **pipe burst** "pipe" phaṭā
bury dafnā
bus bas
bus station bas aḍḍā; bas "station"
bus stop bas "stop"
business tijārat; *work* tijārtī kām
business class tijārtī log; "business" vāle log
businessman tājir
busy masrūf; **I am busy.** Maiṅ masrūf hūṅ.; **The line is busy.** "Line engage" hai.
but lekin
butcher qasā'ī
butterfly titlī
buy xarīd
by: by bus bas se; **by post** post se

C

cabinet *cupboard* almārī; *political* kābīna
cable "cable"
calculator "calculator"
call *verb* bula; **Call the police!** Police ko bula'īye!; **What is that called?** Use kiā kehte haiṅ?
camel ūṅṭ
camera "camera"
camp "camp"; **Can we camp here?** Ham yehāṅ "camp" kar sakte haiṅ?
camping "camp" karna
campsite "camp" karne kī jagah
campus: university campus "university campus"
can *noun* ḍabbā
Canada "Canada"
Canadian "Canadian"
canal neher
cancel mansox; "cancel"; **The plane is canceled.** Havā'ī jahāz "cancel" ho gayā hai.
cancer "cancer"
candle shamā
candlestick mom-battī
candy miṭhā'i; shīrīni
canister kanastar
cannon top
capital *city* dār-ul-hukūmat; rāj dhāni
car "car"
care dekh-bhāl
careful: be careful! dhiyān dīj'ye!
cargo "cargo"
car park "car park"
carpenter baṛhā'ī
carpet qālīn
carrier bag thailī
carry le jā
cart baggī
cartoon "cartoon"
cashier "cashier"
cashier's booth "cashier" kī khiṛkī
cassette "tape"; "cassette"
cast: plaster cast *medical* "plaster"
castle qila
cat billī
catch jhel
cathedral "cathedral"
Catholic "Catholic"
cattle maveshī

c = *church.* **ṅ** = *sing.* **x** = *loch.* **ğ/q** *see p18.* **bh/ch/dh/ḍh/gh/kh/ph/ṛh/th/ṭh** = *breathed.* **ḍ/ṛ/ṭ** = *flapped.*

cauliflower gobhī
cause sabab
cave ğār
CD "CD"
CD player "CD player"
ceasefire jaṅg xatam
cellar teh xānā
cemetery qabrastān
center markaz
century sadī
certain yaqīnī
certainly yaqīnī taur per
chain zanjīr
chair kursī
change *verb* tabdīl kar; **I have to change some dollars.** Maiṅ apne ḍālar tabdīl karnā cāhtā hoṅ
channel "T.V. channel"
chapter sabaq
charity xairātī
charity organization xairātī tanzīm
case peshā
cheap sastā
check *bank* "check"; *verb* dekh; **Check the oil please.** "Oil" kā praishar dekh'ye.
check-in "check-in"
check-in counter "check-in" kī khiṛkī
cheese panīr
chemical "chemical"
chemistry ilm-e-kīmyā
chess shatranj
chest *body* sīnā
chew *verb* cabā
chewing gum cing-gam
chicken murğī
chief sardār
child baccā
children bacce
chin thuḍḍī
China Cīn
Chinese Cīnī
chocolate "chocolate"
choke: He is choking. Us kī sāṅs ghuṭ rahī hai.
cholera "cholera"
choose cun
chop *verb* kāṭ
Christian Īsā'ī
Christianity Īsā'īyat
Christmas "Christmas"
church girjā
cigar "cigar"
cigarette(s) "cigarette(s)"
cigarette papers "cigarette" kā kāğaz
cinema "cinema"
citizen shehrī
citizenship shehrīyat
city shehar
city center shehar kā markaz
city hall shehar kā "hall"
city map shehar kā naqshā
civilian shehrī
civil rights shehrī huqūq
civil war xāna jungī
class *school* "class"
clean *adjective* sāf; *verb* sāf kar
clear *adjective* sāf; khulā
climate mausam
clinic davā xāna
clock ghaṛī
close band kar
clothes kapṛe
clothes shop kapṛe kī dukān
cloud bādal
club "club"
clutch *of car* "clutch"
coal koelā
coal mine koele kī khadān
coast samandar ke qarīb
coat "coat"
code: international code bāhār

a = apple. **ā** = father. **e** = pay. **i** = sit. **ī** = heat. **o** = hotel. **u** = put. **ū** = shoot. **au** = oar. **ai** = pay.

mulk kā fon koḍ
coffee "coffee"
coin sikkā
coins sikke
cold *adjective* ṭhanḍā; *noun* sardī; *medical* zukām; **cold water** ṭhanḍā panī; **I have a cold.** Mujhe zukām hai.; **It is very cold.** Bohut sardī hai.; **I feel cold.** Mujhe sardī lag rahī hai.
colleague sāthī; "colleague"
college "college"
color rang
color film rangīn film
colorless be rang
comb kaṅg-ghā
come ā
comfortable: to be comfortable ārām se
commission: What is the commission? "Commission" kiyā hai?
Commonwealth "Commonwealth"
communications murāsilāt
community qaum
companion sāthī
compare mavāzina kar
comparison mavāzinā
compass qutub numā
compensation ma'āvizā
competition muqāblā
complain shikāyat
computer "computer"
computer virus computer kā "virus"
concussion *medical* jhaṭke
condition hālat
condom "condom"
conference ijlās
confirm: I want to confirm my flight. *m:* Maiṅ apnī "flight" pakkī karnā cāhtā hoṅ./ *f:* Maiṅ apnī "flight" pakkī karnā cāhtī hoṅ.
confusion uljhan
connection ta'aluq
constipation qabz
constitution dastūr
consulate sifārat xhāna
consultant māhir; "consultant"
contact: I want to contact my embassy. Maiṅ apne sifārat xāne se rābta karnā cāhtā hūṅ.
contact lenses "contact lenses"
contain rok thām kar
contemporary maujūdā
contest muqāblā
continue jārī
contract mu'āhidā
control qābū
conversation bāt-cīt
cook *noun* bāvarcī; *verb* pakā
cooker "cooker"
cool ṭhandā
co-operation ta'āvun
copper tāmbā
copy *noun* kāpī; *verb* kāpī kar
corkscrew kork kholne kī cābī
corner moṛ
correct *adjective* sahī; *verb* sahī kar
corruption "corruption"
cost qīmat; **How much does this cost?** Is kī qīmat kiyā hai?
cotton kapās; rū'ī; **cotton wool** rū'ī jā tukṛā
cough *noun* balğam
council "council"
count jama kar
counterfeit jālī; **This money is counterfeit.** Ye paisā jālī hai.
country mulk
countryside dehāt kā ilāqā

c = *church.* **ṅ** = *sing.* **x** = *loch.* **ğ/q** *see p18.* **bh/ch/dh/ḍh/gh/kh/ph/ṛh/th/ṭh** = *breathed.* **ḍ/ṛ/ṭ** = *flapped.*

court *of law* adālat
cow gā'e
craftsman dast kār
crane *machine* "crane"
crash *verb* ṭakkar
craziness pāgal-pan
crazy *adjective* pāgal
create banā
credit qarz; **on credit** qarz per
credit card "credit card"
cricket kriket
crime jurm
criminal mujrim
cross *verb* pār kar
crossing "crossing"
crossroads caurāhā
crow *bird* kavā
cruel zālim
cry *verb: to weep* pukār; cīnx
culture tehzīb
cup peyālī; "cup"
cupboard almārī
cure *noun* shafā; *verb* achchā kar de
currency sikkā rā'ij-ul-vaqt; "currency"
custom *tradition* rivāj
customs *border* "custom"
cut *verb* kāṭ
cut off: I've been cut off. Maiṅ kaṭ gayā hūṅ.; **The electricity has been cut off.** Bijlī kat ga'ī hai.; **The gas has been cut off.** Gais kaṭ ga'ī hai.; **The water has been cut off.** Panī kī lā'in kaṭ ga'ī hai.

D

dairy "dairy"
dam bānd; band
dance *noun* nāc; *verb* nāc
danger xatrā
Dane; Danish Ḍenmārkī
Danish *language* Ḍenish
dark *adjective* tārīk; *color* gehre rang kā
darkness *noun* andherā
date tārīx; **What date is it today?** Āj kiyā tārīx hai?
date of arrival ā'ne kī tarīx
date of birth tarīx-e-paidā'ish
date of departure jāne kī tarīx
daughter laṛkī
dawn *noun* sehr
day din
daytime din kā vaqt
dead marā
deaf behrā
dear *loved* piyāre
death maut
debt qarz
decade das sāl
December Disamber
decide *verb* faislā kar
decision faislā
deep gehrā
deep water gehrā panī
deer hiran
defeat shikast
defend *verb* diffā kar
delay der; **The plane is delayed.** "Plane" der se ā rahā hai.
democracy jamhūrīyat
demonstration *political* siyāsī muzāhirā
dentist dāṅt kā ḍāktar; "dentist"
deodorant "deodorant"
department store "department store"
departures rawānagī
deport "deport" kar
deportation "deportation"
depot "depot"
deprive *verb* mehrūm kar
deprived *adjective* mehrūm

a = apple. **ā** = father. **e** = pay. **i** = sit. **ī** = heat. **o** = hotel. **u** = put. **ū** = shoot. **au** = oar. **ai** = pay.

describe *verb* batā
desert *noun* registān
desire *verb* xāhish kar
desk "desk"
desserts miṭhāī
destroy barbād kar; xātam kar
detergent "detergent"
development taraqī
devil bhot; shaitān
diabetes shakar ki bimārī; "diabetes"
diagnosis *medical* tashxīs
dial *verb* ghūma; ḍā'il kar; **dialing code for London** London ke fon kā koḍ
dialect bol-cāl kī zabān
diaper "nappy"; **I need to change my baby's diaper.** *f:* Maiṅ apnī bacce kī "nappy" badalnā cāhtī hūṅ.
diarrhea "diarrhea"
dictator "dictator"
dictatorship "dictatorship"
dictionary luğat
die *verb* mar
diesel "diesel"
diet *food* ğizā
difference faraq
difficult mushkil
dig *verb* khod
dining car "dining car"
dining room khāne kā kamrā
dinner shām kā khāna
diplomat "diplomat"
diplomatic ties sifārtī ta'aluqāt
direct sīdhā; **Can I dial direct?** *m:* Maiṅ sīdhe fon kar saktā hūṅ?/ *f:* Maiṅ sīdhe fon kar saktī hūṅ?
direction taraf; simt; **Which direction?** Kis taraf?
directory "directory"
dirty gandā
disabled apāhij
disaster sānihā
disco "disco"
discover patā calā
discussion bāt-cīt
disease bīmārī
displaced person be ghar insān
dispute *noun* ixtilāf; jhagṛā
dissolve milā
distance fāslā
distant dūr
district zilā
diver "diver"
divide taqsīm
divorce talāq
dizzy: I feel dizzy. Mujhe cakkar ātā hai.
do kar
doctor ḍāktar
document musavidā; "document"
dog kuttā
doll guṛyā
dollar ḍālar
donkey gadhā
door darvāzā
door lock darvāze kā tāla
double dugnā
double bed baṛā bistar
double room baṛā kamrā
doubt shak
down nīce
drag ghasīṭ
draw nikāl
drawer xāna
dream *noun* xāb
dress *noun* libās
drill *noun* "drill"
drill a hole *verb* sūrāx kar
drink *noun* sharbat; *verb* pī
drinking water pīne kā pānī
drive *verb* calā
driver "driver"

c = *church.* ṅ = *sing.* x = *loch.* ğ/q *see p18.* bh/ch/dh/ḍh/gh/kh/ph/ṛh/th/ṭh = *breathed.* ḍ/ṛ/ṭ = *flapped.*

driver's license "driving license"
drizzle phuvār; **it's drizzling** phuvār paṛ rahī hai
drug *medicine* davā; *narcotics* manshiyāt
drug addict mashiyāt kā nāshā karne vāla
drugstore davā kī dukān
drum ḍhol
drunk *person* sharābī; **to get drunk** sharāb kā nashā kar
duck *noun* batax
during darmiyān meiṅ
Dutch "Dutch"
duty: customs duty kasṭam kī "duty"
duvet raza'ī; lehāf
dwell *verb* reh; bas
dynamo "dynamo"

E

each har
eagle uqāb
ear kān
early jaldī
earnings kamā'ī
earrings bude; jhumke
earth zamīn
earthquake zalzalā
east *noun* mashriq
east(ern) *adjective* mashriqī
easy āsān
eat khā
economics ma'āshiyāt
economist mahir-e-ma'āshiyāt; "economist"
economy *of country* ma'īshat
editor mudīr
education tālīm
egg anḍā
eight āṭh
eighteen aṭhāra
eighty asī
elbow kuhnī
elder *adjective* baṛā
elect muntaxib kar
election intixāb
electrical goods store biglī ke sāmān kī dokān
electricity bijlī
elevator lift
eleven giyāra
e-mail "e-mail"
e-mail address "e-mail" kā patā
embassy sifārat xānā
emergency "emergency"
emergency exit "emergency" darvāza
empty *adjective* xālī; *verb* xālī kar
end *noun* xātam; *verb* xātam kar
enemy dushman
engine "engine"
engineer ingīniar
England Bartāniyā
English *person* Angrez; *thing/language* Angrezī
enough kāfī; bas; **That's enough.** Kāfī hai.
enquiry pūch-tāch
enter dāxil
entire pūrā
entrance dāxla
envelope lifā-fā
epidemic vabā
epilepsy mirgī
equal barābar
equality barābrī
equipment sāmān
era daur
escape *verb* bac
especially xās tor per
essay mazmūn
establish qā'im kar

a = apple. **ā** = father. **e** = pay. **i** = sit. **ī** = heat. **o** = hotel. **u** = put. **ū** = shoot. **au** = oar. **ai** = pay.

etiquette ādāb
euro *currency* "euro"
Europe "Europe"
European "European"
European Union "European Union"
evening shām
every har
everybody; everyone her ek
everything har cīz
evidence subot
exactly bilkul
exam imtihān
examine *medically* jāṅc
example misāl
excellent behtarīn
except ke alāva
excess *adjective* ziyāda
exchange *verb* tabdīl; **Do you exchange money?** Āp paisā tabdīl karte haiṅ
excuse *noun* bahāna
exercise kasrat
exhaust *of vehicle* "silencer"
exhibit *verb* numā'ish kar
exhibition numā'ish
exit *noun* nikalne kā rāsta; *verb* nikal
expect umīd kar
expel jilā vatan kar
expensive meṅhgā
explain vāzih kar
explanation vazāhat
explode phaṭā
exploration khoj; talāsh
explosion dhamākā
explosives dhamākā-xez ashyā; barūd
export *noun* bar āmad; *verb* bar āmad kar
express *fast* tez raftār
extend baṛhā
extra ziyāda; **an extra blanket** ek ziyāda "blanket"
eye āṅkh; **eyes** āṅkhaiṅ
eyeglasses cash'mā
eyesight nazar

F

face *noun* cehrā
fact haqīqat
factory kārxāna
failure nākāmī
fall *verb* gir
false *adjective* jhūtā
family xāndān
famous mashhūr
fan paṅkhā
fan belt gāṛī ke paṅkhe kā bailṭ
far dūr; **How far is the next village?** Aglā gā'oṅ kitnī dor hai?
fare kirāya; **What is the fare?** Kirāya kitnā hai?
farm farm
farmer kisān
farming khetī-bāṛī
Farsi Fārsī
fashion "fashion"
fast *quick* jaldī; tezī se; *verb:* **I am fasting.** Maiṅ roze se hūṅ.
fat *adjective* moṭā
father abbā
fax faiks
fax machine "faiks machine"
fear *noun* ḍar; xauf; *verb* ḍar lag
February Farvarī
federation "federation"
feed *verb* khilā
feel lag; mehsūs kar
female māda
fence bāṛh; "fence"
ferret neyvla
ferry kashtī; nā'o

fertile zarxez
fertilizer khād
festival tehvār; **film festival** filmī tehvār
feud adāvat; puranī dushmanī
fever buxār
field maidān
fifteen pandrā
fifty pacās
fight *noun* jhagṛā; *verb* laṛ
fighter laṛne vāla
file *paper/computer* "file"
fill bhar; **to fill in a form** "form" bhaṛye
film film
film festival filmī tehvār
filmmaker film-sāz
filter *noun* chan-nī
final *adjective* āxrī; *noun* āxhrī
financial mālī
find *verb* talāsh kar; **to find out** *verb* patā kar
fine *adjective* achchā; *adverb* achchī tareh se; *noun: penalty* jurmāna
finger unglī
finish *verb* xatam kar
fire āg
firewood jalane kī lakṛī
first pehlā/pehlī
first class pehlā darjā
fish machlī
fishing machlī pakaṛnā
five pańc
fix muqarrar
flash *verb* camak
flashlight "flashlight"
flea kīṛā
flee bhāg
flight uṛān
float *verb* tair
flock jhunḍ; kharo
flood sailāb
floor *ground* farsh; *story* manzil; **on the floor** farsh per
florist phūl vāla/phūl valī
flour āṭā
flower phūl
flu buxār
fly *noun* kīṛā; *verb* uṛā
fog kuhar
foggy kuhar ālūd
folk *noun* desī; **folk dancing** rivāyatī nāc; **folk music** rivāyatī mosīqī
folklore rivāyatī bāteṅ
food khāna
fool *noun* budh-dhū
foot pā'oṅ; *measurement* fūṭ
football "football"
footpath "footpath"
forbid manā kar
forbidden manā
foreign ğair mulkī
foreigner ğair mulkī
forest "jungle"
forget bhūl jā
fork kāṭa
form *shape* banāvat; **application form** darxāst kā fārm
fort qilā
fortnight do hafte
forty cālīs
forum "forum"
forwards āge
foundation bunyād
four cār
fourteen caudā
fourth cauthā
fracture *noun* "fracture"
France "France"
free *adjective* xālī; *liberated* āzād; *of charge* muft; **Is this seat/taxi free?** Ye sīṭ/tāksī xālī hai?
freedom āzādī

freeze jamā hūvā
freezing shadīd sard; barfelī
freight *noun* kirāya
French Fransīsī
fresh tāza
Friday Jumma
fridge "fridge"
friend dost
frighten xof zadā
frog meṅḍak
front *noun* āge; **in front of** ke āge
frontier sarhad
frost baraf bārī
fruit phal
fruit juice phal kā ras
fuel īṅdhan
fuel dump tel kā cirāğ
full bharā; **full moon** pūrā cānd; **I am full up!** Merā paiṭ bhar gayā hai!
funeral janāza
funny ajīb-o-ğarīb
furniture "furniture"
future mustaqbil

G

gallon "gallon"
game khel
game park shikār kā jaṅgal
gangrene "gangrene"
garage "garage"
garden bāğ
garbage kacrā
garlic thom
gas "gas"; *for car* "petrol"
gas bottle gas kī botal
gate "gate"
gear *of car* "gear"
general *adjective* ām
genitals tanāsulī
genocide qatl-e-ām
geologist "geologist"
German "German"
Germany Germany
germs jarāsīm
get hāsil kar; lā
gift tohfā
ginger adrak
girl laṛkī
girlfriend "girlfriend"
give birth paida kar
give de
glass *substance* shīshā; *for drinking* "glass"; **glass of water** panī kā "glass"; **eyeglasses** cash'mā
gloves dastāne
go jā; **let's go!** jā'eṅ!
goal *aim* maqsad; *football* gol
goat bakrī
God Xudā; Allāh
gold sonā
golf golf
good achcha
good-bye! xudā hāfiz!
government hukomat
grain dāna
gram "gram"
grammar qavā'id
granddaughter potī
grandfather dādā
grandmother dādī
grandson potā
grape angūr
grass ghāṅs
grateful: I am grateful. Maiṅ shukr guzār hūṅ.
grave *serious* baṛī; *noun* qabar
gravel bajrī
great azīm
greatest sab se azīm
Greece Yūnān
Greek Yūnānī
green harā

c = *church.* **ṅ** = *sing.* **x** = *loch.* **ğ/q** *see p18.* **bh/ch/dh/ḍh/gh/kh/ph/ṛh/th/ṭh** = *breathed.* **ḍ/ṛ/ṭ** = *flapped.*

greengrocer sabzī vāla
grind pīs
ground zamīn
group ṭolī
grow *verb* baṛh; *crops* lagā; ugā
grown-up baṛā
guard *noun* caukīdār; *verb* hifāzat kar
guest mehmān
guesthouse "guesthouse"
guest speaker muqarir mehmān
guide *verb* rehnumā'ī kar
guidebook "guidebook"
gum *mouth* masūṛā
gun bandūq
gynecologist "gynecologist"

H

hair bāl
hairbrush bal kā barash
hairdresser nā'ī
hair-dryer bāl sūkhāne kī mashīn
half ādhā
hammer hathūṛā
hand hāth
handbag "handbag"
handicraft dast-kārī
handle "handle"
hand over de-de; supurd kar
hang *verb* laṭkā
hangar "hangar"
happy xush
hard *not soft* saxt; *difficult* mushkil
harmful nuqsān de
harvest fasal
hat "hat"
hate *verb* nafrat kar
hatred nafrat
have *see page 14.*
have to zarūrī; vājbī
he vo
head sar; *boss* sardār; **head of state** sadar
headache sar dard
headquarters markaz
heal achchā ho
healing shafā
health sehat
healthcare hifzān-e-sehat
healthy sehat mand
hear sun
heart dil; qalb
heart attack dil kā daura
heat *noun* garmī; *verb* garam kar
heaven jannat
heavy bhārī
helicopter "helicopter"
hell dozax
hello! salām alekum!; *response* vālekum salām!
help *noun* madad; *verb* madad kar; **Can you help me?** Āp merī madad kar sakte haiṅ?
hen murğī
hepatitis pīliā; "hepatitis"
her us kā
herb jaṛī-būṭī
herd ğol
here yahāṅ
herself vo xud
hidden chupā
hide *verb* chup
high oṅcā; **high blood pressure** "high blood pressure"
highway shāh rāh
hijack *verb* iğvā kar
hijacker iğva'ī
hijacking iğvā
hike *noun* baṛhat; *verb* lambī ser
hill pahāṛ
him us
himself vo xud
Hindi Hindi

a = apple. **ā** = father. **e** = pay. **i** = sit. **ī** = heat. **o** = hotel. **u** = put. **ū** = shoot. **au** = oar. **ai** = pay.

Hindu Hindu
Hinduism Hindū maz-hab
hire *verb* kirā'e per le
his us kā
historian mo'arix
history tārīx
hit mār
hold *verb* pakaṛ
hole sūrāx
holiday chuṭṭī
homeland vatan
homeless be ghar
honey shaihid
honeymoon *noun* "honeymoon"
hood *of vehicle* gāṛī kā huḍ
hook huk
horse ghoṛā
horse racing ghoṛe kī res; "horse racing"
horse-riding ghorā savāṛī
hose baṛā pā'ip; "hose"
hospital haspatāl
host mezbān
hostage iğvā kunindagān; **to take hostage** iğvā karnā
hostel "hostel"
hot garam; **hot water** garam panī; **It is hot.** Garamī hai.
hotel "hotel"
hour ghantā
house ghar
how kaise; **how far?** kitna dūr?; **how many?** kitne sāre?; **how much?** kitnā?
however al-batta
human *adjective* insānī
human being insān
human rights insānī huqūq
humanitarian insānī falāh
humanitarian aid insānī falāh kī imadad; insānī madad
humor mazāq
humorous mazāqī
hundred sau
hungry bhūkā; **I'm hungry.** Maiṅ bhūkā hūṅ.
hunt *verb* talāsh
hurry jaldī
hurt dard; **Where does it hurt?** Kahaṅ per dard hai?; **It hurts here.** Yehaṅ per dard hai.
husband shauhar; xāvind
hygiene safā'ī

I

I maiṅ
ice baraf
ice-cream "ice-cream"
I.D card shanaxtī kārḍ; **Do you have any I.D.?** Āp ke pas shanaxtī kārḍ hai?
idea xiyāl
identification pehcān
if agar; **if possible** agar mumkin ho
ill bīmār; **I am ill.** Maiṅ bīmār hūṅ.
illegal nā jā'iz
illness bīmārī
image "image"
immigrant muhājir
immigration *noun* hijrat
import *noun* dar āmad
importance ahmīyaṭ
important aihim
impossible nā mumkin
improve ṭhīk kar
in meiṅ; **in front of** us ke sāmne
included shāmil
independence xud muxtār
independent state xhud muxtār mulk
India Hindustān
Indian Hindustānī
indicator light "indicator light"

c = *church.* ṅ = *sing.* x = *loch.* ğ/q *see p18.* bh/ch/dh/ḍh/gh/kh/ph/ṛh/th/ṭh = *breathed.* ḍ/ṛ/ṭ = *flapped.*

indigestion bad hazmī
industry "industry"
infant nauxaiz
infection "infection"
influenza "influenza"
information malūmāt
information office malūmātī daftar; "information office"
injure zaxmī kar
injured zaxmī; **to be injured** zaxmī hūnā
injury zaxam
ink siyāhī
inner-tube andarūnī nālī
innocent masūm; be gunāh
insane pāgal
inscription naqsh
insect kīṛā; **insects** kīṛe
insecticide kīṛe mārne kī davā
instead ke bajā'e
institute idāra
insurance "insurance"; **I have medical insurance.** Mere pās tibbī "insurance" hai.
insured: My possessions are insured. Maira sāmān "insured" hai.
intend irāda kar
intention irāda
interest dil casbī; *financial* sūd
interesting dil casb
interior andar kā
internal andarūnī
international code bainul aqvāmī "phone code"
international flight bainul aqvāmī "flight"
international operator bainul aqvāmī "operator"
internet internet
interpreter tarjumān
interval vaqfā
interview "interview"
into ke andar; meiṅ
introduce *to someone* ta'aruf kar
introduction ta'aruf
invasion hamlā
invention ījād
inventor ījād karne vāla
investigate taftīsh kar
investigation taftīsh
invitation dāvat
invite dāvat de
Iran Irān
Iranian Irānī
Ireland "Ireland"
Irish "Irish"
iron *for clothes* istarī
Islam Islām
Islamic Islāmī
it vo
Italian "Italian"
Italy "Italy"
itch *noun* khujlī

J

jack *of car* "jack"
jacket sadrī; "jacket"
January Janvarī
Japan Jāpān
Japanese Jāpānī
jaw jabṛā
jazz "jazz"
jeans "jeans"
jewelry zevar; *gold* sone kā zevar; *silver* cāndī kā zevar
Jew; Jewish person Yahūdī
Jewish Yahūdī
job kām; naukrī
joke *noun* mazāq; latīfā; *verb* mazāq kar
journalist sahāfī
Judaism Yahūdīyat

a = apple. **ā** = father. **e** = pay. **i** = sit. **ī** = heat. **o** = hotel. **u** = put. **ū** = shoot. **au** = oar. **ai** = pay.

judge qāzī; "judge"
July Julā'ī
June Jūn
junior chotā
justice insāf

K

kebab kabab
keep rakh
ketchup caṭnī
kettle ketlī
key cābī
kidnap iğvā kar
kidnapper iğvā karne vāla
kidnapping iğvā
kidney gurda
kill mār; qatal kar
killer qātil
kilogram kilo
kilometer kilomiter
kind *adjective* rehim-dil; *noun: type* qism; tarah
king bādishāh
kiosk kā'ūnṭar
kitchen bāvarcī xāna
knee ghuṭnā
kneel jhuk
knife cāqū
know: I know. Maiṅ jāntā hūṅ.; **I don't know.** Maiṅ nahīṅ jāntā.
knowledge mālūmāt
known: well-known mashhūr
Koran Qurān

L

laboratory "laboratory"
lack *noun* kamī
ladder sīṛhī
lake jhīl
lamb dumbā; bheṛ
lamp cirāğ
land *noun* zamīn; *verb* utar
landslide zamīn kā khisaknā
language zabān
lap god
laptop *computer* "laptop"
large baṛā
last āxrī
late der se
laugh *verb* haṅs
laughter haṅsī
laundry *clothing* maile kapṛe; *place* dhobī kī dūkān
law qānūn
law court adālat
lawyer vakīl
lay rakh
lazy kāhil; sust
lead *noun* baṛhat
lead *verb* qiyādat kar
leader qā'id
leadership qiyādat
leaf pattā
leak "leak"
lean *adjective* dublā; *verb* jhuk
leap *verb* kūd
leap year līp kā sāl
learn sīkh
leather camṛā
leave *verb* choṛ
lecture dars; "lecture"
left *side* bāyāṅ
left-wing "communist"
leg ṭāṅg
legal qānūnī
legend shāh kār
lemon nībū; līmū
lend qarz de
length lambā'ī
lengthen baṛhā
lens "lens"; **contact lenses** "contact lenses"
less kam

lesson sabaq
letter *written* xat
lettuce patta-gobhī
level *adjective* barā-bar; "level"; *noun* satah
lever līvar
liberation āzādī
library "library"
liberty āzādī
lice jūṅ
lie *noun* jhūṭ
lie down leṭ jā
life zindagī
lift *noun: elevator* "lift"; *verb* uṭhā
light *adjective: not dark* ujāla; raushnī; *not heavy* halkā; *noun* raushnī; *electric* bijlī; *verb* jalā; **Do you have a light?** Āp ke pass sigraiṭ kī lā'it hai?; **to light a fire** āg jalā
light bulb bijlī kā "bulb"
lighter "lighter"
light meter "light" kā mīṭar
lighting roshānī
lightning biglī kaṛaknā
like ke jaisā; **like that** us ke jaisā; **like this** is ke jaisā; *verb* pasand kar
likely: to be likely mumkin hai
limbs hāth-pā'oṅ
lime *fruit* nībū
limit had
line "line"
linguist mahir-e-lisāniyāt
linguistics ilm-e-lisāniyāt
lip hoṅṭ
lipstick "lipstick"
list fahrist
listen sun
literature adab
litter kacrā
little thoṛā; **a little bit** thoṛā sā
live ṭhahr
liver jigar; kalejā
lizard chipkalī
loaf ek rotī
local pās kī; **local shop** pās kī dūkān
location jagā
lock *noun* tālā; *verb* tālā lagā
locomotive koele kā ingin
long lambā
look dekh
look for kī talāsh
loose change chuṭṭe
loss nuqsān
lot: a lot bohut sārā
loud zor kī āvāz
loudly zor se
louse jūṅ
love *noun* piyār; muhabbat; *verb* piyār kar
low nīcā; **low blood pressure** "low blood pressure"
luck qismat
lunch dopehar kā khānā
lungs phaipṛe

M

machete churā
machine machine
madrasa madrasā
magazine parcā
magnetic "magnetic"; maqnātīsī
mail ḍāk
mailbox ḍāk ka ḍabbā
main aslī; "main"; **main square** baṛā corāhā
maintain dek-bhāl
majority aksarīyat
make banā
make-up "make-up"

a = apple. **ā** = father. **e** = pay. **i** = sit. **ī** = heat. **o** = hotel. **u** = put. **ū** = shoot. **au** = oar. **ai** = pay.

male nar
mammal dūdh vāly jānvar
man insān
manager "manager"
many bohut; ka'ī; **too many** bohut sāre; **how many?** kitne
map naqshā; **map of Pakistan** Pākistān kā naqsha
march *noun* morcā
March *month* Mārc
mark nishān
market bāzār
marriage shādī
married: I am married. Maiṅ shadī shudā hūṅ.
marsh daldal kā ilāqa
martyr shahīd
mascara kājal
match *football* "match"
matches *plural* diya salā'i
material māl
mathematics hisāb
matter: It doesn't matter. Ko'ī bāt nahīṅ hai.
mattress gadda
mausoleum dargāh
maybe shā'id
me maiṅ
meal khāna
meals khāne
mean: What does that mean? Is kā kiā matlab hai?
meaning matlab
measure *verb* nāp-tol
meat gosht
mechanic "mechanic"
media "media"
medical tibbī; "medical"
medical insurance tibbī "insurance"
medicine davā'ī
meet mill
meeting mulāqāt
melon tarbūz; xarbūz
member vafd; "member"
memory yāddāsht
menu "menu"
message payām; paiğām
metal dhāt
meter *measure* "meter"; **light meter** "light" kā "meter"
middle bīc; **in the middle** bīc meiṅ
midnight ādhī rāt
midwife āyā
mile mīl
military *adjective* faujī; *noun* fauj
milk dūdh
mill āṭe kī cakkī
million "million"
minaret minārā
mine *mineral* khadān
minefield "minefield"
miner "miner"
mineral water mā'da'nī-yātī pānī; "mineral water"
minister vazīr
ministry vazrāt; **Ministry of Agriculture** Vazrāt-e-Zirā'at; **Ministry of Defence** Vazrāt-e-Difā; **Ministry of Education** Vazrāt-e-Tālīm; **Ministry of Foreign Affairs** Vazrāt-e-Xārja; **Ministry of Health** Vazrāt-e-Sehat; **Ministry of Justice** Vazrāt-e-Insāf/Adal
minority aqalliyat
minute *noun* minaṭ
miracle mojizā
mirror ā'īnā
Miss "Miss"
missile "missile"
mist shabnam
mistake *noun* ğaltī; **to make a mistake** ğaltī kar

model "model"
modem "modem"
modern jadīd; "modern"
moment lamhā; vaqt
monarch hākim
Monday Pīr
money paisā
month mahīna
monument yadgār
moon cānd; **new moon** nayā cānd; **full moon** pūrā cānd
more aur; ziyāda; **more or less** taqrīban; lag-bhag
morning subah; āj subah
mosque masjid
mosquito machchar
most sab se ziyāda
mother māṅ
motorbike "motorcycle"
motorway shāh rāh; "motorway"
mountain pa'hāṛ
mouse cūhā
mouth mūṅ
move *verb* hil
movement harkat
movie "film"
Mr. Janāb
Mrs. Begam
Ms. Muhtarimā
much ziyāda; **too much** bohut ziyāda; **not much** ziyāda nahīṅ; **how much?** kitnā?; **how much is it?** ye kitne kā kitnā hai?
mud kī'caṛ
mule xaccar
murder *noun* xūn; *verb* xhūn; qatal kar
murderer qatil
museum ajā'ib ghar
music mūsīqī
Muslim *person* Musalmān
moustache mūṅch
must zarūrī; vājbī
mustard rā'ī
my merā
myself maiṅ xud

N

nail nāxun; **finger nail** unglī kā nāxun
nail-clippers nāxun kāṭne kī mashīn; "nail cutter"
name nām; **surname** xāndanī nām; **What is your name?** Āp kā nām kiyā hai?; **My name is Emma.** Mairā nām Emma hai.
napkin "napkin"
nappy "nappy"; **I need to change my baby's nappy.** *f:* Maiṅ apnī bacce kī "nappy" badalnā cāhtī hūṅ.
narrow taṅg
nation *state* mulk
national mulkī
nationality shehrīyat
natural qudratī; **natural resources** qudratī zarā'e
nature qudrat
navy behrī fauj
near qarīb
nearby ās-pās; qarīb meiṅ
nearly taqrīban
necessary zarūrī; **it's necessary** ye zarūrī hai
neck gardan
necklace "necklace"
necktie ṭā'ī
need zarūrat
needle sū'ī; **Do you have needle and thread?** Āp ke pās sū'ī aur dhāga hai?
negotiator bāt-cīt karne vālā
neighbor paṛosī
neither ko'ī bhī nahīṅ

a = apple. **ā** = father. **e** = pay. **i** = sit. **ī** = heat. **o** = hotel. **u** = put. **ū** = shoot. **au** = oar. **ai** = pay.

nerve āsb; nas; rag
net: fishing net maclī pakaṛne kā jāl; **mosquito net** machchar dānī
never kabhī nahīṅ
new nayā; **new moon** nayā cānd; **New Year** ṇayā sāl
New Zealand "New Zealand"
news xabar
newspaper axbār; **newspaper in English** Angrezī axbār
next dūsrā; **next week** agle hafte
nice achcha
night rāt; **good night!** shab baxair!
night club "night club"
night guard; night watchman rāt kā caukidār
nine nau
nineteen unnīs
ninety navve
no nahīṅ; **no entry** dāxla mamnū; **no smoking** tambakū noshī manā hai; **no sugar** binā shakar
nobody ko'ī nahīṅ
noise shor-o-ğul
noon dopeher
normal ṭhīk; ām
north *noun* shumāl
north(ern) shumālī
Northern Ireland Shumālī "Ireland"
nose nāṅk
not nahīṅ; mat
note: banknote bank kā not
notebook kāpī
nothing kuch nahīṅ
nought sifar
noun nām
novel novel"; **novel in English** angrezī novel
now ab; **right now** abhī
nowhere kahīṅ nahīṅ
number "number"
nurse "nurse"

O

obligation farz
observer dekhne vāla
occupation *job* peshā; *of a country* qabzā
occupying forces qābiz fauj
occur ho
October Aktūbar
of kā
office daftar
often aksar
oil *cooking* khane kā tel; mineral "oil"; **oil can** tel kā ḍabba; **oil pipeline** oil kī "pipeline"; **oil production** oil nikālnā; **oil refinery** "oil refinery"; **oil spill** oil kā phailnā; **oil tanker** oil kā "tanker"; **oil well** oil kā kūvāṅ; **oil field** kī kān
old *person* baṛā; *thing* purānā; **How old are you?** Āp kī umar kiyā hai?; **I am ... years old.** Merī umar ... sāl hai.
on per; **on time** vaqt per; **Is the train on time?** Traiṅ vaqt per hai?
once ek dafā
one ek
one-way street ek taraf saṛak
one-way ticket ek taraf kā ṭikiṭ
only *adjective* sirf; *adverb* sirf
onto *preposition* per
open *adjective* khulā; *verb* khol
operating theater/room "operation theater"
operation *surgical* amal-e-jarāhī; "operation"

c = *church.* ṅ = *sing.* x = *loch.* ğ/q *see p18.* bh/ch/dh/ḍh/gh/kh/ph/ṛh/th/ṭh = *breathed.* ḍ/ṛ/ṭ = *flapped.*

operator calāne vāla; **telephone operator** "telephone operator"
opposite sāmne
opposition muxālifat
or yā
orange *fruit* santarā; *color* narangī; bhagvā
orchard phal kā bāğ
order *verb* hukm de; **to order a meal** khane kā āḍar de
ordinary ām
origin asal; ibtidā
original aslī
orphan yatīm
orphanage yatīm xāna
other dūsrā
ounce chaṭāk; "ounce"
our hamāra
ourselves ham xud
out bāhar; **to go out** bāhar jā
outside bāhar
overcoat "overcoat"
overtake *verb* āge nikal
owl ullū
own *adjective* apnā; xhud kā
owner mālik
oxygen "oxygen"

P

padlock zanjīr kā tālā
pain dard; taklīf
painkiller dard kī davā
paint *noun* "paint"; *verb* "paint"; rang kar
painter "painter"
painting "painting"
Pakistan Pākistān
Pakistani *person* Pākistānī; *thing* Pākistānī
palace mehal
pale *color* halkā rang
paper *substance* kāğaz; newspaper axbār; **a piece of paper** kāğaz kā tukṛā
parachute "parachute"
paradise jannat
paralyze maflūj
parcel "parcel"
parents vālidain
park *noun* bāğ; *verb* kharī kar
parliament aivān; "parliament"
part hisā
participate hisā le; shāmil ho
party taqrīb; "party"; *political* "party"
pass *noun* kāmiyāb; pas; *verb* de
passable: Is the road passable? Is saṛak se jā sakte haiṅ?
passenger musāfir
passport "passport"; **passport number** "passport" kā nambar
past *adjective* māzī kā; purānā; *noun* purānā daur
pasta "pasta"
path rāstā
patience sabar; *medical* marīz
patient: to be patient sabar kar
pay *noun* tanxā; *verb* de
payment raqam
pay phone "public phone"
peace aman; **peace-keeping troops** amnī fauj; **peace talks** amnī muzākirāt
peak cotī; **mountain peak** pahaṛ kī cotī
pearl motī
pediatrician baccoṅ kā ḍāktar
pediatrics baccoṅ kī ḍāktarī
pelvis jāṅgh
pen qalam
pencil "pencil"
penicillin "penicillin"
penknife chotā cāqū; qalam

a = apple. **ā** = father. **e** = pay. **i** = sit. **ī** = heat. **o** = hotel. **u** = put. **ū** = shoot. **au** = oar. **ai** = pay.

kā cāqū
people log
pepper kalī mirc
perfect bilkul sahī
perform adā kar
performance *arts* adā-kārī; *work* kām
performer adā kār
perfume itr; "scent"
perhaps shā'id
period *of time* vaqt; daur; *menstrual* māhvārī; haiz
Persian Irānī; *language* Fārsī
person shaxs
petrol petrol
pharmacy davā'ī kī dūkān
phone *noun* "phone"; *verb* "phone" kar
photo tasvīr
photocopier zīrāks kī mashīn
photocopy *noun* zīrāks kāpī; *verb* kāpī kar; *verb* kāpī banā
photographer musavir; "photographer"
photography musavirī; "photography"
physics ilm-e-tibbīyāt
physiotherapy "physiotherapy"
piano "piano"
pickax kudāl
picture tasvīr
pig sūvar; xinzīr
pill golī
pillow takyā
pilot "pilot"
pin "pin"
pink gulābī
pipe *tube* "pipe"; *smoking* huqa
pistol pistaul; tamancā
pitch *football* fūṭbal kā meṅdān
pizza "pizza"
place jagā; **place of birth** paidāish kī jagā
plain *noun* sāda
plane *airplane* hava'ī jahāz
plank ballī
plant *noun* paudā; *verb* lagā
planting pauda lagānā
plastic "plastic"
plate rakābī
platform "platform"
platform number "platform number"
play *noun: theater* drāma; *verb* khel
pleasure mazā
plow *noun* hal; *verb* jot
plug *electric* palag
plum alūcha; zard ālu
p.m. shām
poach *animals* corī se shikār
poacher *of animals* corī se shikār karne vāla
pocket jeb
podium cabūtrā
poem nazam
poet shā'ir
poison zaihar
police police
policeman police vāla
police station thānā; "police station"
polite narm; tamīz dār
political siyāsī
politician siyāsat dāṅ
politics siyāsat
polo "polo"
pony xaccar
poor ğarīb
population ābādī
pork sūvar kā gosht
port bandargāh
portion hisā
possible mumkin; **Is it possible?** Ye mumkin hai?
position *noun* hālat

c = *church.* **ṅ** = *sing.* **x** = *loch.* **ğ/q** *see p18.* **bh/ch/dh/ḍh/gh/kh/ph/ṛh/th/ṭh** = *breathed.* **ḍ/ṛ/ṭ** = *flapped.*

post office dāk xāna
postcard "postcard"
potato ālū
pottery cīnī ke bartan
pound *weight/sterling* "pound"
pour ḍāl
powder pāuḍar
power tāqat
praise *verb* tārīf kar
pray du'ā kar
prayers namāz
prefer ziyāda pasand kar
pregnant hāmilā; **I'm pregnant.** Maiṅ hāmilā hūṅ.
prepare tayār kar
preparation tayārī
present *time* hāl; *gift* tauhfā
president sadar
presidential guard sadar kā "guard"
press *noun: news* "press"; *verb* dabā; *verb* zor lagā
pressure zor; "pressure"; **high blood pressure** high blood pressure"; **low blood pressure** "low blood pressure"
previously pehle
price qīmat
pride ghamanḍ; ğurūr
priest pādrī
prime minister vazir-e-āzam
print chāp
printer *computer* "printer"
prison jel; qaid
prisoner qaidī
prisoner-of-war jangī qaidī
prize inām
probable mumkin; shā'id
problem maslā; **no problem!** kūī maslā!; bāt nahīṅ!
product tayār-shuda māl; "product"
profession peshā
professional *person* peshavar
program: radio program "radio" kā program; **computer program** "computer" kā program
projector "projector"
pronounce *verb* ailān kar
pronunciation talafuz
proof subūt
protect *verb* hifāzat kar
protection hifāzat
protest *noun* aihtijāj; *verb* aihtijāj kar
proud ghamandī; mağrūr
prove sābit kar
proverb kahāvat
pub "pub"
public phone "public phone"
publish chāp
publisher *company* chāpā xāna; idāra-e-ishā'at
pull khaiṅc
pump *noun* "pump"; *verb* "pump" kar
pumpkin kaddū
puncture "puncture"
punish *verb* sazā de
pupil shāgird
purple baignī
push *noun* dhakka
put *verb* rakh; **to put on clothes** kapṛe pehaṅye

Q

quarter *of city* ilāqa
quarter *fourth* cauthā'ī; **one-quarter** ek cauthā'ī; **three-quarters** tīn cauthā'ī
queen rānī
question savāl
quick jald

a = apple. **ā** = father. **e** = pay. **i** = sit. **ī** = heat. **o** = hotel. **u** = put. **ū** = shoot. **au** = oar. **ai** = pay.

quickly jaldī se
quiet *adjective* xāmūsh
quietly xāmūshī se
quilt razā'ī
quilt gadda
quit choṛ
Quran Qurān

R

rabbit xargosh
rabies pāgal kutte ke kāṭne kī bīmārī
radar "radar"
radiator "radiator""
radio "radio"; **radio broadcast** "radio" nashriyāt; **radio program** "radio program"; **radio station** "radio station"
raid acānak hamlā; "raid"
railway "railway"
railway station "railway station"
rain *noun* bārish; **It is raining.** Bārish ho rahī hai.
rainbow qos-e-qazah; dhanak
raise *verb* uṭhā
Ramadan Ramzān
range: mountain range pahaṛī ilāqa
rape zanā bil jabar
rapid jaldī-jaldī
rapidly jaldī se
rat cūhā
rate qīmat
ravine khā'ī
raw kaccā
razor; razorblade "razor"
reaction rad-e-amal
read paṛh
reading paṛhā'ī
ready teyār; **I am ready.** Maiṅ teyār hūṅ.
real aslī
reality haqīqat
realize samajhā
reaping fasal kāṭnā; phal pānā
reason sabab; vajeh; **for that reason** us vajeh se; **reason for travel** safar karne kī vajeh
rebel *noun* bāğī
receipt rasīd
receive milā
recently hāl meiṅ
reception desk "reception"
recognize *verb* pehcān
record *noun: lp* "record"; likhā paṛhā'ī; **world record** ālamī "record"; *verb* rikauḍ kar
red surx
referee "referee"
refinery "refinery"
refrigerator firig
refugee muhājir; **refugees** muhājirīn; **refugee camp** muhājiroṅ kā "camp"
region ilāqa
registered mail "registered" ḍāk
reign *noun* daur-e-hukūmat
relationship ta'aluqāt
relatives rishte dār
relax ārām
release *verb* choṛ
relief aid imdād
religion maz-hab
remain mau'jūd
remember yād kar
repair *noun* ṭhīk karnā; joṛnā; *verb* ṭhīk kar; joṛ
repeat *verb* dohrā; phir se kar
replace tabdīl kar
reply *noun* javāb; *verb* javāb de
report "report"
represent numā'indagī kar
representation numā'indagī
representative numā'inda
republic "republic"

research tehqīq
reservation "reservation"; **I have a reservation.** Mairā "reservation" hai.
reserve: game reserve shikār kā ilāqa
reserve *verb*: **Can I reserve a place/seat?** *m:* Maiṅ sîṭ "reserve" kar saktā hūṅ?/ *f:* Maiṅ sīṭ "reserve" kar saktī hūṅ?
rest *noun* ārām; *remainder* bacā hūvā; *verb* ārām kar
restaurant "restaurant"
return *noun* vāpasī; **return ticket** vāpasī kā ṭikiṭ
revenge badlā
reverse *verb* "reverse" kar
review *in newspaper* tabsirā
revolution bağāvat
rice cāval
rich amīr
ride a horse ghuṛ savārī
rifle bandūq
right *side* dāyaṅ; sīdhā; *correct* sahī
rights huqūq; **civil rights** shehrī huqūq; **human rights** insānī huqūq
ring *noun* gherā; aṅghūtī
riot *noun* fasād
ripe pakā
rise uṭh
risk *noun* xatrā; *verb* xatrā le
river nadī; **river bank** nadī kā kināra
road saṛak; **road map** saṛak kā naqshā; **road block** rāste kī rukāvaṭ; **road sign** "road sign"
rob lūṭ; **I have been robbed.** Mujhe lūṭ liyā hai.
robbery ḍākā
rock caṭān
rocky caṭānī
roof chat
room kamrā; **single room** choṭa kamrā; **double room** baṛā kamrā; **room number** kamre kā nambar; **room service** kamre kī "service"
rope rasī
rosary tasbīh
rose gulāb kā phūl
roundabout corāha
route rāstā
row *line* qatār
royal shāhī
rubber "rubber"
rubbish kacrā
rude bad tamīz
rug choṭā qālīn
rugby "rugby"
ruins khanḍar
ruler *person* hākim; *measure* iskel
run *verb* bhāg;
run out xatam; **I have run out of gas.** Merī gais xatam ho ga'ī hai.
Russia Rūs
Russian Rūsī
rust zang

S

sack *noun* thailā; borā; *verb* chuṭṭī kar
sad ğamgīn; udās
safe *adjective* mehfūz
safety hifāzat
safety pin "safety pin"
sailing bādbānī safar; "sailing"
sailboat bādbānī kashtī
saint valī
salad salād

a = apple. ā = father. e = pay. i = sit. ī = heat. o = hotel. u = put. ū = shoot. au = oar. ai = pay.

salesperson "sale" vāla
salon: beauty salon "beauty salon"
salt namak
salty namkīn
sand ret
sandwich "sandwich"
satellite "satellite"
satellite phone "satellite" kā fon
satisfactory itmenān baxsh
satisfied mutma'in
Saturday Hafta
sausage "sausage"
save *rescue* bacā; **to save money** paisā bacā
saw *noun* ārī
say keh
scarf dupaṭṭā
scatter bikhrā hūvā
school maktab; "school"
science sā'ins
scientific sā'insī
scientist sā'ins dāṅ
scissors qaiṅcī
score *verb* "score" kar; **What's the score?** "Score" kiyā hai?; **Who scored?** Kis ne "score" kiyā?
Scot "Scot"
Scotland "Scotland"
Scottish "Scottish"
screw *noun* "screw"
screwdriver peṅc-kash
scythe haṅsyā
sea samandar
search *verb* talāsh
season mausam
seat nāshist; "seat"; *political* nāshist
second *adjective* dūsrā; *noun* dūsrā
second-hand purāna; istīmāl shudā
secret *adjective* xufyā; *noun* xufyā
section hisā
security hifāzat
see dekh
seed dāna
seek talāsh kar; justajū kar
sell beṅc
send bhej
senior purāna; baṛā
sense samajh; hosh; **common sense** ām samajh
sensible hoshyār
September Sitambar
series silsila
serious *adjective: grave* xarāb
service "service"
session nashist
seven sāt
seventeen satrā
seventy sattar
several ka'ī
severe shadīd; **severe heat** shadīd garmī
sew sī
sewing machine sīne kī mashīn
sex *act* suhbat; mubashirat; jamā; *gender* jins
sexual jinsī; **sexual relations** jismānī ta'aluqāt
shade sāyā
shake *verb* hilā; milā
shampoo shaimpū
shape banāvaṭ
share *noun* hisā; *verb* ke sāth
sharp tez
shaving cream "shaving cream"
she vo
sheep bheṛ
sheet cādar
shell *from sea* sīpī; *military* golā
shelter mahfūz jagā
shepherd gadaṛyā

c = *church.* ṅ = *sing.* x = *loch.* ğ/q *see p18.* bh/ch/dh/ḍh/gh/kh/ph/ṛh/th/ṭh = *breathed.* ḍ/ṛ/ṭ = *flapped.*

shine camak
ship panī kā jahāz
shirt qamīs
shock *medical* "shock"; jhaṭkā; **electric shock** biglī kā jhaṭkā
shoe jūtā; **shoes** jūte
shoe shop jūte kī dūkān
shoot golī mār; **Don't shoot!** Golī mat mārye!
shop dūkān
shopkeeper dūkān dār
shopping xarīdārī
shore kināra; **sea shore** samandar kā kināra
short kam; muxtasar; *height* ṭhiṅgnā
shortage kamī; qilat
shoulder kandhā
shout *verb* cillā
shovel phā'oṛā
show *noun* khel; *verb* dikhā
shower *bath* "shower"; *rain* halkī barish
shut *verb* band kar
sick bīmār; **I am sick.** Maiṅ bīmār hūṅ.
sight nazar
sign *noun* nishān; *verb* dastaxat kar
signature dastaxat
significance ahmīyat; no'īyat
significant ahim
sign language ishāroṅ kī zabān
Sikh Sīkh
silence xāmūshī
silent xāmūsh
silk resham
silly bevaqūf; aihmaq
silver cāndī
similar ek jaisā
since jab se; tab se
sing *verb* gā
single akelā
sink *noun* "sink"; *verb* dūb
sister behen
sit baiṭh
situation hālat
six che
sixteen sola
sixth chaṭā
sixty sāṭh
size nāp; "size"
skiing "skiing"
skill hunar
skilled hunar-mand
skin jild; camṛī
sky āsmān
sleep *verb* so
sleeping bag sone kā beg
sleeping car "sleeping car"
sleeping pills nīnd kī golī
sleepy: to feel sleepy nīṅd āna
sleet baraf-bārī
sling *medical* "plaster" kī paṭṭī
slip *verb* phisal
slope utār; ḍhalān
slow dhīre
slowly dhīre dhīre
small choṭā
smell *noun* bū
smoke *noun* dhūvāṅ
smoking sigreṭ pīnā
smuggler ismagalar
snack halkā phulkā khānā
snake sāṅp
snake bite sāṅp kā kāṭā
snow barf bārī; **It is snowing.** Barf bārī ho rahī hai.
so much/many itne sāre
soap sābun
soccer fūṭbāl
soccer match fūtbāl kā maic
social samājī; ma'āshiratī
society samāj; ma'āshirat
sock mozā
soft naram

a = apple. **ā** = father. **e** = pay. **i** = sit. **ī** = heat. **o** = hotel. **u** = put. **ū** = shoot. **au** = oar. **ai** = pay.

soldier faujī
solve hal nikāl; hal kar
some kuch
somehow kisī tarah se
someone/somebody ko'ī
something ko'ī cīz
sometimes kabhī-kabhī
somewhere kahīṅ per
son laṛkā
song gānā
soon jaldī
sore throat xarāb galā
sorry: I'm sorry! mujhe māf kaṛye!
soul rūh
sound āvāz
soup sābun
sour kaṛvā
source zaryā
south *noun* junūb
south(ern) junūbī
souvenir yādgār
sow *verb* bo
space xalā
spade kudāl
Spanish Hispānvī
spanner pānā
spare tire isṭaipnī
sparkle camak
speak bol; **Do you speak English?** Āp English bolte haiṅ?; **I speak Urdu.** Maiṅ Urdū boltā hūṅ.
speaker muqarir
specialist "specialist"
spectacles cash'mā
speed raftār
spelling hijje
spend xarc kar
spicy *hot* masāla dār; taiz; mircī vāla
spider makṛī
spill chalak
spin ghumā
spine *back* raiṛh kī haḍḍī
spit *verb* thūk
splint *medical* plāstar
split *verb* alag kar; alag ho
spoil *verb* barbād kar
sponge "sponge"
spoon camcā
sports khail kūd
sportsman khilāṛī
spread phailā
spring *season* bahār; *of water* panī kā cashmā; *metal* "spring"
spy jāsūs
square corāha; **town square** shehar kā corāha
stadium "stadium"
staff *employees* "staff"; mulāzimīn
stage "stage"
stale bāsī
stallion nar ghoṛa
stamp *postal* ḍāk tikiṭ; *official* mohur
stand *noun* "stand"; *verb* khaṛā ho
star sitāra
state *nation* mulk; *in federation* riyāsat; *condition* hālat
station "station"
stationery "stationery"
statue mujasamā
stay ṭhair
steal *verb* curā; *and see* **stolen**
steel *noun* faulād
steering wheel gaṛī kā hainḍal
sterling "pound"
stethoscope daktar kā āla
stick *noun* lakṛī; *verb* cipkā
still *adverb* phir bhī; tab bhī
sting *verb* kāṭ
stink *verb* bad-bū

c = *church.* **ṅ** = *sing.* **x** = *loch.* **ğ/q** *see p18.* **bh/ch/dh/ḍh/gh/kh/ph/ṛh/th/ṭh** = *breathed.* **ḍ/ṛ/ṭ** = *flapped.*

stitches *surgical* ṭāke
stolen corī kā; **My wallet has been stolen.** Merā pars corī ho gayā hai.; **My car has been stolen.** Merī kār cūrī ho gaī hai.
stomach peṭ
stomach ache peṭ kā dard
stone path-thar
stop *something* ruk; *someone* rok; **stop!** ruk'ye!
store *for storage* godām; *shop* dūkān; *verb* rakh
storm tūfān
story kahānī; *floor* manzil
stove "stove"
straight sīdhā; **straight on** sīdhe; **Go straight ahead.** Sīdhe jā'īye.
strange ajīb-o-ğarīb
stranger ajnabī
stream jharnā
street saṛak
strength qūvat
stretcher "stretcher"
strike *noun: from work* haṛtāl; *verb* mār
string ḍor; rasī
strong mazbūt
structure banāvaṭ
struggle jad-o-jehad
stuck: Our car is stuck. Hamāri gāṛī phass ga'ī hai.
student talib-e-ilm
study *noun* paṛhā'ī; *verb* paṛh
subject mazmūn
suburb muzāfāt
success kāmyābī
such aisā
suddenly acānak
sufficient kāfī
sugar shakar; cīnī
suit *of clothes* "suit"
suitable mauzūṅ; ṭhīk
suitcase "suitcase"
summer garmī kā mausam
summit cotī
sun sūraj
sunblock cream "sun cream"
Sunday Itvār
sunglasses ḍhūp kā cashmā
sunny: It is sunny. Ḍhūp hai.
sunrise tulū āftāb
sunset ğurūb āftāb; sūraj ḍhalnā
supermarket "supermarket"
supper shām kā khānā
supplies "supplies"
supply *verb* "supply"
sure *adjective* yaqīn; **I am sure.** Mujhe yaqīn hai.
surely *adverb* yaqīnī tor per
surf *noun* jhāg
surgeon "surgeon"; jarāh
surgery *operation* amal-e-jarāhī; "operation"
surname xandānī nām
surprising ta'ajub xez
survey *noun/verb* "survey"
surveyor "surveyor"
swallow *verb* nigal
swamp daldali ilāqa
sweat *verb* pasīna bahā
sweater "sweater"
sweep jhāṛ
sweet *adjective/noun* mīṭhā
swim tair
swimming tairnā
swimming pool tairne kā pūl; "swimming pool"
swimsuit tairne ke kapṛe; "swimsuit"
swing *noun* ghumā
switch *electric* bijlī kā baṭan; "switch"
switch off band kar
switch on khol

a = apple. **ā** = father. **e** = pay. **i** = sit. **ī** = heat. **o** = hotel. **u** = put. **ū** = shoot. **au** = oar. **ai** = pay.

symbol nishān
symptom alāmat; taklīf
syntax tarkīb
syringe "syringe"
system nazm; tarīqā

T

table mez
tablecloth dastar-xān
tablet golī
take le
take-away/-out food ghar lejāne kā khāna
take off uṛān bhar; **What time does the plane take off?** Hava'ī jajāz kitne baje uṛe gā?
talk *noun* bāt-cīt; *verb* bāt kar
tall lambā
tank ṭeṅk
tap *faucet* ṭoṅtī
tape tep
tape-recorder "tape-recorder"
taste *noun* mazā; *verb* cakh
tasteless be-mazā
tasty lazīz
tax *noun* "tax"
tax-free binā "tax"
taxi "taxi"
tea cā'e; **tea with lemon** nībū kī cā'e; **tea with milk** dūḍh kī cā'e
teach paṛhā
teacher ustād
team "team"
tear *verb* phāṛ
tears āṅsū
teaspoon cā'e kā camac
technical taknīkī
technique taknīk
teeth dāṅt
telecommunications "telecommunications"
telegram "telegram"
telephone *noun* "telephone"; fon; **satellite phone** "satellite phone"; *verb* "telephone" kar
telescope dūrbīn
television television
telex tār
tell keh
temperature darja-e-harārat; **I have a temperature/fever.** Mujhe buxār hai.
temple mandir
ten das
tennis tenis
tent tambū; shamīyāna
tenth dasvāṅ
termite xatam kar
terrible bohut burā
territory ilāqa
test *noun* jāṅc
text ibārat
than se
thank you! āp kā shukriyā!
that *pronoun* vo; *preposition* ke
theater "theater"
theft corī
their unkā
them unke
themselves vo xud
then phir
theory "theory"
there vahaṅ
therefore is līye
thermometer "thermometer"
these ye
they vo
thick *wide* cauṛā; moṭa; **thick forest** ghanā jaṅgal
thief cor
thin patlā; dublā
thing cīz; **things** cīzeṅ
think *verb* soṅc

third *adjective* tīsrā; **one-third** ek tihā'ī
thirsty piyāsa; **I am thirsty.** Maiṅ piyāsa hūṅ.
thirteen terā
thirty tīs
this ye
those vo
thought xiyāl
thousand hazār
thread dhāga; **Do you have needle and thread?** Āp ke pās sū'ī aur dhāga hai?
three tīn
three times; thrice tīn dafā
throat galā
thrombosis xūn jamnā
throne taxt
through pār
throughout āxir tak
throw pheṅk
thumb aṅghūṭā
thunder biglī kī kaṛak
Thursday Jumerāt
ticket ṭikiṭ; **one-way ticket** ek taraf kā ṭikiṭ; **return ticket** vāpsi kā ṭikiṭ; **ticket office** ṭikiṭ ghar
tie *verb* bāndh
ties: diplomatic ties sifāratī ta'aluqāt
tights "tights"
time vaqt; **three times** tīn dafa; **for a long time** kāfi vaqt se; **free time** fursat kā vaqt; **What time is it?** Kiyā vaqt hai?
timetable auqāt; "timetable"; **timetable for travel** safār kā "timetable"
tire *noun* "tire"
tired thakā; **I am tired.** Maiṅ thakā hūvā hūṅ.
tiredness thakāvaṭ
tiring thakāne vāla
tissues "tissues"
toast *bread* tost
tobacco tambākū
today āj
toe pā'oṅ kā paṅja
together sāth; ek sāth
toilet bait-ul-xalā; pāxāna
toilet paper "toilet paper"
toiletries "toiletries"
tomato ṭamāṭar
tomb mazār
tomorrow kal; **day after tomorrow** parsoṅ
tongue zabān
tonight āj rāt
too bhī; **too little** bohut thoṛā; **too little** zarā sā; **too many/much** bohut sārā
tools pāne; "tools"
tooth dāṅt
toothache ḍāṅt kā dard
toothbrush ḍāṅt kā barash
toothpaste ḍāṅt kā manjan; "toothpaste"
toothpick xilāl
top ūpar
torture *noun* azīyat; *noun* "torture"
tourism siyāhat; "tourism"
tourist office "tourist office"
tourist sa'īyāh
tow: Can you tow us? Āp ise ṭo kar sakte haiṅ?
tow rope "tow" karne kī rasī
towel tauliyā
tower minārā
town shehar; **town center** shehar kā markaz
track pagḍanḍī
tractor "tractor"
trade union "trade union"

a = apple. **ā** = father. **e** = pay. **i** = sit. **ī** = heat. **o** = hotel. **u** = put. **ū** = shoot. **au** = oar. **ai** = pay.

tradition rivāj; rivāyat
traditional rivāyatī
traffic lights traffic kī lā'iṭ
traffic police "traffic police"
train rail gaṛī
train station rel gaṛī kā isṭeshan; "train station"
tranquilizer behoshī kī davā
transfer flights bdalne vālī flā'iṭs; "transfer flights"
transformer "transformer"
transfusion: blood transfusion xūn denā
translate tarjumā kar
translation tarjumā
translator tarjumān
transmit muntaqil kar/de
transmitter "transmitter"
transport zara-e-haml-o-naqal; "transport"
trap *verb* jāl
trash fuzūl
trauma sadmā
travel *noun* safar; *verb* safar kar
travel agency "travel agency"
traveler musāfir; **travelers** musāfirin
traveler's check "travel check"
treacherous dağā-bāz
treasury "treasury"
tree jhāṛ
trial *legal* muqaddamā; *test* azmā'ish
troops sipāhī
trouble paraishānī; mushkil; **What's the trouble?** Kiyā mushkil hai?
trousers patlūn; pants
truce salāh
truck "truck"; lāṛī
true sac
trunk *of car* dikkī; būṭ
truth saccā'ī
try koshish kar
tube nalkī
Tuesday Maṅgal
tunnel suraṅg
Turk Turkī
Turkey Turkī
Turkish Turkī
turn *noun: in road* moṛ; *verb* muṛ
twelve bāra
twenty bīs
twice do bār
twins jurvān
two do
type *noun* qism; tarah
typewriter "typewriter"; "typing machine"
tyre *noun* "tyre"

U

ulcer phoṛā; "ulcer"
umbrella chatrī
uncle *see page 98.*
uncomfortable taklīf-de
under *preposition* niche; *adverb* ke asar meiṅ; ke tehat
underground zamīn doz
understand *verb* samjhā; **Do you understand?** Āp samajhte haiṅ?; **I understand.** Maiṅ samajhtā hūṅ.; **I don't understand.** Maiṅ nahīṅ samajhtā hūṅ.
undertake hāth meiṅ lenā
underwear caḍḍī; "underwear"
unemployed be-rozgār
unemployment be-rozgārī
unfortunately bad-qismatī se
unhappy nā xush
unification ittihād
uniform *noun* "uniform"

c = *church.* **ṅ** = *sing.* **x** = *loch.* **ğ/q** *see p18.* **bh/ch/dh/ḍh/gh/kh/ph/ṛh/th/ṭh** = *breathed.* **ḍ/ṛ/ṭ** = *flapped.*

union *noun* "union"; **trade union** "trade union"
unique apne āp meiṅ ek
United Nations Aqvām-e-Muttahida
United States of America Riyāsat-e-Muttahida-e-Amarīkā
university "university"
unknown gum-nām
unless jab-tak
until jab-tak
up ūpar
U.S.A. "U.S.A."
use *noun/verb* istemāl
useful kār-āmad
usually ām taur per

V

vacation chuṭṭī
vaccinate ṭīkā lagā
vaccinated ṭīkā lagā hūvā; **I have been vaccinated.** Mujhe ṭīkā lagā hūvā hai.
valley vādī
van "van"
varnish lakṛī kā pālish; "varnish"
vase gul-dastā
vegetables sabzī; **vegetable shop** sabzī kī dūkān
vegetarian sabzī xor; **I am a vegetarian.** Maiṅ sabzī xor hūṅ.
vein rag
venereal disease jinsī bīmārī
verb fe'l
very bohut
veto "veto"
vice-president nā'ib sadar
victim mazlūm
victory fatah
video cassette "video cassette"
video player "video player"
view *noun* nazāra; manzār
village dehāt; gā'oṅ
vinegar sirkā
violence tashaddud
virus "virus"
visa "visa"
visit *verb* jā
visitor mehmān
voice āvāz
vomit qe; **I need to vomit.** Mujhe qe ā rahī hai.
vote *noun* "vote"; *verb* "vote" de

W

wages rozī
wait intizār kar
wait for kā intizār; **Please wait for me.** Merā intizār kaṛye.
waiter waiter
wake *up* uṭh; **Please wake me up.** Mujhe uṭhā'īye. **Please wake Kevin up.** Kevin ko jagā'īye.
Wales Wales
wall dīvār
wallet baṭvā; purse
want cāh; **I want some water.** Mujhe panī cāhī'ye.; **I don't want this.** Mujhe ye nahīṅ cāhī'ye.
war jang; **civil war** xānā-jangī
warm garam
wash *verb* dho
washing powder/detergent kapṛe dhone kā pauḍar
watch *noun* ghaṛī; *verb* dekh; nazar rakh
watchmaker's ghaṛī-sāz
water pānī; **Is there any water?**

a = apple. **ā** = father. **e** = pay. **i** = sit. **ī** = heat. **o** = hotel. **u** = put. **ū** = shoot. **au** = oar. **ai** = pay.

Vahaṅ pānī hai?
water bottle panī kī botal
waterfall ābshār
watermelon xarbūz; tarbūz
wave *sea* mauj
way rāstā; **this way** is taraf; **that way** us taraf; **which way?** kis taraf?
we ham
weak kamzor
weapon hathyār
wear *verb* pehan
weather mausam
Wednesday Budh
week haftā; **last week** pichle hafte; **next week** agle hafte; **this week** is hafte
weekend "weekend"
weep *verb* ro
weight vazan
welcome xush āmded
well *adjective* achchā; *adverb* achchī tareh; *noun* kūvaṅ
well-known mash-hūr
Welsh "Welsh"
west *noun* mağrib
western *adjective* mağribī
wet *adjective* gīlā; bhīgā
what? kiyā?
what kind of? kis tarah kā?
what is that? vū kiyā hai?
wheat gehūṅ
wheel cakkā
wheelchair "wheelchair"
when? kab?
where? kahāṅ?
where from? kahāṅ se?
where is? kahaṅ hai?
where are? kahāṅ haiṅ?
which? kaun sā?
while jab ke
whisky "whisky"
white safaid
who kaun
whole pūrā
why? kiyoṅ?
wide caur'ā
wife bīvī
win *noun* jīt; *verb* jīt; **Who won?** Kaun jītā
wind *noun* havā
window khir'kī
windy havā'ī
wine sharāb
wing per
winter sardī kā mausam
wire tār; **barbed wire** xardār tār
wisdom samajh dārī
wise *adjective* samaj dār
with sāth
withdraw nikāl
without bağair; binā
witness *noun* gavāh
wolf bhair'yā
woman aurat
womb batan; baccā dānī
wood *substance* lakr'ī; *forest* choṭā jangal
wool ūn
work *noun* kām; *verb* kām kar; **I work in a bank** Maiṅ bank meiṅ kām kartā hūṅ.; **This phone doesn't work.** Ye fon kām nahīṅ kartā.
worker kām karne vālā
world duniyā
worried fikir-mand; paraishān
worry *verb* fikir kar; paraishān ho; **Don't worry!** Fikir mat karye!
worse sab se burā
worthy lā'īq
wound *noun* zaxam
wrap *verb* lapeṭ; **Would you like it wrapped?** Kiyā āp lapeṭ kar leṅ ge?

c = *church.* **ṅ** = *sing.* **x** = *loch.* **ğ/q** *see p18.* **bh/ch/dh/ḍh/gh/kh/ph/ṛh/th/ṭh** = *breathed.* **ḍ/ṛ/ṭ** = *flapped.*

wrench *tool* pāna
wrestling pehilvānī; kushṭī
wrist kalā'ī
write likh
writer musanif
writing likhā'ī; **writing paper** likhne kā kāğaz
wrong: This is wrong. Ye ğalat hai.; **You are wrong!** Āp ğalatī per haiṅ!

X

X-rays "X-rays"

Y

yard *measurement* gaz; *garden* āṅgan
year sāl; **last year** pichle sāl; **next year** agle sāl; **this year** is sāl
yellow pīlā
yes hāṅ
yesterday kal; **the day before yesterday** parsoṅ
yet: not yet abhī tak nahīṅ
yield *noun* paida-vār; fasal
yogurt dahī
you *singular* āp; *plural* āp log
young choṭā
young person javān
your; yours *singular* āp kā; *plural* āp ke
yourself āp xud
yourselves āp log xud
youth *noun* javānī

Z

zero sifar
Zoroastrian Pārsī; Ātish Parast; Zartash
zoo cur'yā ghar

URDU
Phrasebook

1. ETIQUETTE

Greetings are given greater prominence in Urdu than English, and there is a wide variety not only of greeting formulas — varying according to time and occasion — but also the set responses to them. A general "hello!" is **ādāb arz!**, to which the response is the same. A Muslim greeting for use by someone of any religion for any time of the day is **as-salāmu alaikum!** ("peace be upon you!") to which the response is **(va) alaikum as-alām!** ("and to you peace!"). Hindus also use **namaste!** which means both "hello!" and "goodbye!" (in a similar manner to the Italian "ciao!"), and **dhanyāvād!** "thank you!" There is not the same emphasis in Urdu on time-specific greetings such as "good morning" and "good evening". Here are some other common exchanges you'll encounter:

how are you?	**āp kaise haiṅ?**
fine, thanks!	**āp kī duā hai!**
pleased to meet you!	**āp se milkar baṛī xushī hū'ī!**
goodbye!	**xudā hāfiz!**
see you later!	**phir mileṅge!**
please!	**meharbānī karke!***
thank you!	**shukriya!**
thank you very much!	**bahut shukriya!**
not at all!	**koi bāt nahīṅ!**
excuse me!; sorry!	**(mujhe) māf karye!**
congratulations!	**mubārāk(bād)!**
welcome!	**xush āmaded!**
bon voyage!	**safar mubārak ho!**

* Note, however, that "please" is more usually implied in the polite form of the request itself.

2. QUICK REFERENCE

yes	**hāṅ**
no	**nahīṅ**
I	**maīṅ**
you *polite/plural*	**āp (log)**
he/she/it	**vo**
we	**ham**
they	**vo**
this/these	**ye**
that/those	**vo**
here	**yahāṅ**
there	**vahāṅ**
is there?/are there?	**kyā vahāṅ hai/haiṅ?**
where is/are . . . ?	**kahāṅ hai/haiṅ?**
where?	**kahāṅ?**
who?	**kaun?**
what?	**kyā?**
when?	**kab?**
which?	**konsā?**
how?	**kaise?**
why?	**kiyoṅ?**
how far?	**kitnā dūr?**
how near?	**kitnā qarīb?**
how much?	**kitnā?**
how many?	**kitne?**
what's that?	**vo kyā hai?**
very	**bohut**
and	**aur**
or	**yā**
but	**lekin**

c = *church.* **ṅ** = *sing.* **x** = *loch.* **ğ/q** *see p18.* **bh/ch/dh/ḍh/gh/kh/ph/ṛh/th/ṭh** = *breathed.* **ḍ/ṛ/ṭ** = *flapped.*

I like . . .	**Mujhe . . . pasand hai.**
I don't like . . .	**Mujhe . . . pasand nahīṅ hai.**
I want . . .	**Mujhe . . . cāhīye.**
I don't want . . .	**Mujhe . . . nahīṅ cāhīye.**
I know.	**Mujhe patā hai.**
I don't know.	**Mujhe patā nahīṅ.**
Do you understand?	**Āp samajhte haiṅ?**
I understand.	**Maiṅ samajhtā hūṅ.**
I don't understand.	**Maiṅ nahīṅ samajhtā hūṅ.**
I am sorry (to hear that).	**Mujhe afsos hai.**
I am grateful.	**Maiṅ shukur guzār hūṅ.**
It's important.	**Ye ahim hai.**
It doesn't matter.	**Ko'ī bāt nahīṅ.**
No problem!	**Ko'ī bāt nahīṅ!**
more or less	**taqrīban**
Here is . . .	**Yahāṅ . . . hai.**
Here are . . .	**Yahāṅ . . . haiṅ.**
Is everything OK?	**Sab ṭhīk hai?**
Danger!	**Xatra!**
How do you spell that?	**Āp ise kaise likhte haiṅ?**
I am . . .	
cold	**Mujhe sardī lag rahī hai.**
hot	**Mujhe garmī lag rahī hai.**
sleepy	**Mujhe nīnd ā rahī hai.**
hungry	**Mujhe bhūk lag rahī hai.**
thirsty	**Mujhe piyās lag rahī hai.**
angry	**Mujhe ğusa ā rahā hai.**
happy	**Maiṅ kush hūṅ.**
sad	**Maiṅ ğam zadā hūṅ.**
tired	**Maiṅ thakā hūṅ.**
well	**Maiṅ achchā hūṅ.**

a = apple. **ā** = father. **e** = pay. **i** = sit. **ī** = heat. **o** = hotel. **u** = put. **ū** = shoot. **au** = oar. **ai** = pay

—Regional nationalities

Afghanistan	**Afghanistān**
—Afghan	**—Afghāni**
Bangladesh	**Banglādesh**
—Bangladeshi	**—Banglādeshī**
Burma	**Burma**
—Burmese	**—Burmī**
Nepal	**Nepal**
—Nepalese	**—Nepalī**
Bhutan	**Bhutan**
—Bhutanese	**—Bhutanī**
Tibet	**Tibat**
—Tibetan	**—Tibat kā**
Sri Lanka	**Sri Lanka**
—Sri Lankan	**—Sri Lankan**
Tajikistan	**Tajikistān**
—Tajik	**—Tajikistānī**

—Occupations

What do you do?	**Āp kyā karte haiṅ?**
I am a/an . . .	**Maiṅ . . . hūṅ.**
academic	**mahir-e-tālīm**
accountant	**"accountant"**
administrator	**munazim**
aid worker	**imdādī kārkun**
architect	**"architect"**
artist	**fankār**
banker	**"banker"**
business person	**"business" vālā**
carpenter	**baṛhā'ī**
civil servant	**sarkārī nokar**
consultant	**"consultant"**
dentist	**"dentist"** *or* **dāṅt kā ḍāktar**

c = *church.* **ṅ** = *sing.* **x** = *loch.* **ğ/q** *see p18.* **bh/ch/dh/ḍh/gh/kh/ph/ṛh/th/ṭh** = *breathed.* **ḍ/ṛ/ṭ** = *flapped.*

designer	**"designer"**
diplomat	**"diplomat"**
doctor	**dāktar**
economist	**"economist"**
engineer	**injinīr**
factory worker	**"factory" meṅ kām karne vāla**
farmer	**kisān**
filmmaker	**film banāne vāla**
journalist	**sahāfī**
lawyer	**vakīl**
mechanic	**"mechanic"**
nurse	**"nurse"**
officer worker	**"office" meṅ kām karne vālā**
pilot	**"pilot"**
scientist	**sā'ins-dāṅ**
secretary	**"secretary"**
soldier	**faujī**
student	**tālib-e-ilm**
surgeon	**"surgeon"**
teacher	**ustād**
tourist	**sa'īyah**
writer	**musanif**

I work in . . .	**. . . maiṅ kām kartā hūṅ.**
advertising	**ishtihār** *or* **"advertising"**
computers	**"computers"**
insurance	**"insurance"**
I.T.	**"I.T."**
the leisure industry	**"leisure industry"**
marketing	**"marketing"**
an office	**daftar**
the retail industry	**"retail industry"**
sales	**"sales"** *or* **baicne kā kām**

a = *apple*. **ā** = *father*. **e** = *pay*. **i** = *sit*. **ī** = *heat*. **o** = *hotel*. **u** = *put*. **ū** = *shoot*. **au** = *oar*. **ai** = *pay*.

a shop	**dūkān**
telecommunications	**"telecommunications"**
tourism	**"tourism"**
the hotel industry	**"hotel industry"**

—Age

How old are you?	**Āp kī umar kyā hai?**
I am . . . years old.	**Merī umar . . . hai.**

—Family

Are you married?	**Āp shadī-shuda haiṅ?**
I am single	**Maiṅ ğair shadī-shuda hūṅ.**
I am married.	**Maiṅ shadī-shuda hūṅ.**
I am divorced.	**Merī talāq ho ga'ī hai.**
I am widowed.	**Maiṅ bevā hūṅ.**

Do you have a boyfriend?	**Āp kā "boyfriend" hai?**
Do you have a girlfriend?	**Āp kī "girlfriend" hai?**
What is his/her name?	**Us kā nām kyā hai?**
How many children do you have?	**Āp ke kitne bacce haiṅ?**
I don't have any children.	**Mere bacce nahīṅ.**
I have a daughter.	**Merī ek laṛkī hai.**
I have a son.	**Merā ek laṛkā hai.**

How many sisters do you have?	**Āp kī kitnī behneṅ haiṅ?**
How many brothers do you have?	**Āp ke kitne bhā'ī haiṅ?**

children	**bacce**
daughter	**laṛkī**
son	**laṛkā**
twins	**juṛvāṅ**
husband	**shohar** *or* **xāvind**

c = *church.* **ṅ** = *sing.* **x** = *loch.* **ğ/q** *see p18.* **bh/ch/dh/ḍh/gh/kh/ph/ṛh/th/ṭh** = *breathed.* **ḍ/ṛ/ṭ** = *flapped.*

wife	**bīvī**
family	**xāndān**
man	**ādmī**
woman	**aurat**
boy	**laṛkā**
girl	**laṛkī**
person	**shaxs**
people	**log**

—Religion

Official statistics report that around 97 percent of the population of Pakistan is Muslim of which 77 percent is Sunni and 20 percent Shi'i. There are also groups of various sizes such as Hindus, Sikhs and Christians, and the Zoroastrian Parsees. Every town in the country has at least one large mosque where Muslims congregate for the Friday prayer, and some are wonderful examples of early and modern Islamic architecture. Pakistan is also home to many impressive Buddhist and Hindu monuments, a reminder of the country's rich religious heritage.

What is your religion?	**Āp kā maz-hab kyā hai?**
I am (a) . . .	**Maiṅ . . . hūṅ.**
Muslim	**Musalmān**
Sikh	**Sikh**
Hindu	**Hindu**
Buddhist	**Buddhist**
Christian	**Īsā'ī**
Catholic	**Kātolikī**
Jewish	**Yahūdī**
Zoroastrian	**Parsī**
I am not religious.	**Maiṅ maz-habī nahīṅ hūṅ.**

4. LANGUAGE

Aside from other indigenous languages spoken in Pakistan, almost everyone knows at least a few words of Arabic (this comes from both studying at Koranic school as well as popular cultural influences). English is also widespread but this depends from area to area. In many places, particularly the larger ports and cities, people will also know a smattering of languages like Persian. Depending on the region, Urdu will share space with languages such as Panjabi, Pashto, Sindhi, Baluchi and Siraiki. As pointed out in the Introduction, there is little problem in understanding Hindi.

Do you speak English?	**Āp ko English ātī hai?**
Do you speak Hindi?	**Āp ko Hindī ātī hai?**
Do you speak German?	**Āp ko German ātī hai?**
Do you speak Italian?	**Āp ko Italian ātī hai?**
Do you speak French?	**Āp ko Fransisī ātī hai?**
Do you speak Spanish?	**Āp ko Spanish ātī hai?**
Do you speak Farsi?	**Āp ko Fārsī ātī hai?**
Do you speak Arabic?	**Āp ko Arabī ātī hai?**
Does anyone speak English?	**Ko'ī English boltā hai?**
I speak a little . . .	**Maiṅ thoṛī-thoṛī . . . boltā hūṅ.**
I don't speak . . .	**Maiṅ . . . nahīṅ bolta.**
I understand.	**Maiṅ samajhtā hūṅ.**
I don't understand.	**Maiṅ nahīṅ samjhā.**
Could you speak more slowly, please?	**Āp dhīre bol sakte haiṅ?**
Could you repeat that?	**Phir se bolye?**
How do you say . . . in Urdu?	**Urdū meṅ isāy kaise bolte haiṅ?**

c = *church.* **ṅ** = si*ng.* **x** = lo*ch.* **ğ/q** *see p18.* **bh/ch/dh/ḍh/gh/kh/ph/ṛh/th/ṭh** = *breathed.* **ḍ/ṛ/ṭ** = *flapped.*

What does . . . mean?	**. . . kā kyā matlab hai?**
How do you pronounce this word?	**Ise kaise kehte haiṅ?**
Please point to the word in the book.	**Kitāb maiṅ vo lafz batā'īye.**

I speak . . .	**Mujhe . . . ātī hai.**
Arabic	**Arabī**
Danish	**Danish**
Dutch	**Dutch**
English	**English**
Farsi	**Farsī**
French	**Fransisī**
Hindi	**Hindi**
German	**German**
Italian	**Italian**
Japanese	**Jāpānī**
Spanish	**Hispanvī**

5. BUREAUCRACY

name	**nām**
surname	**xandānī nām**
address	**patā**
date of birth	**tarīx-e-paidā'ish**
place of birth	**jagah paidā'ish**
nationality	**shehrīyat**
age	**umar**
sex: male	**mard**
female	**aurat**
religion	**maz-hab**
reason for travel:	**safar karne kī vajeh:**
business	**tijārat**
tourism	**siyāhat**
work	**kām**
personal	**zātī**
profession	**pesha**
marital status:	
single	**ğair shādī-shudā**
married	**shādī-shudā**
divorced	**talāq-shudā**
date	**tarīx**
date of arrival	**āne kī tarīx**
date of departure	**jāne kī tarīx**
passport	**pāsporṭ**
passport number	**pāsporṭ kā nambar**
visa	**visa**
currency	**sikka** *or* **rupyā**

c = *church.* **ṅ** = *sing.* **x** = *loch.* **ğ/q** *see p18.* **bh/ch/dh/ḍh/gh/kh/ph/ṛh/th/ṭh** = *breathed.* **ḍ/ṛ/ṭ** = *flapped.*

—Getting around

What does this mean?	**Is kā kyā matlab hai?**
Where is . . .'s office?	**. . . kā "office" kahāṅ hai?**
Which floor is it on?	**Kis manzil per hai?**
Does the elevator work?	**Ye lift kām kartī hai?**
Is Mr/Ms . . . in?	**. . . Sahib/Sāhiba haiṅ?**
Please tell him/her that I have arrived.	**Un ko batā'īye maiṅ ā geā hūṅ.**
I am here.	**Maiṅ yahāṅ hūṅ.**
I can't wait, I have an appointment.	**Maiṅ intizār nahīṅ kar saktā, mujhe aur bhī kām hai.**
Tell him/her that I was here.	**Un ko batā'īye maiṅ āyā thā.**

More on family...

Urdu has a wide range of specialized words for family members. Some of the more common are:

grandfather *paternal*	**dādā**
grandfather *maternal*	**nānā**
father	**vālid; bāp**
mother	**vālida; māṅ**
uncle *paternal*	**cacā**
uncle *maternal*	**māmūṅ**
aunt *paternal*	**phūpī**
aunt *maternal*	**xālā**
brother	**bhā'ī**
sister	**bahin**
nephew *brother's son*	**bhatījā**
niece *brother's daughter*	**bhatījī**
nephew *sister's son*	**bhāṅjā**
niece *sister's daughter*	**bhāṅjī**

6. TRAVEL

PUBLIC TRANSPORT — Local travel is provided by numerous taxis, auto-rickshaws (**rikshā**), minibuses, and horse-drawn two-wheeled carts known as **tongas**. Travel between cities and towns is provided by vans, buses and coaches with the better ones offering air-conditioning. Pakistan also has an extensive railway network connecting the major cities, and trains have first-class and air-conditioned carriages. You'll have to book ahead before catching your train. Air is also an option with regular flights to major cities. The major domestic carrier is PIA, although there are private airlines that serve several cities.

What time does . . . leave/arrive?	**. . . kab jāta/ātā hai?**
the airplane	**havā'ī jahāz**
the boat	**kashtī**
the bus	**bas**
the train	**rel gāṛī**
The plane is delayed.	**Havā'ī jahāz leṭ hai.**
The plane is canceled.	**Havā'ī jahāz "canceled" ho geā hai.**
The train is delayed.	**Rel gāṛī leṭ hai.**
The train is canceled.	**Rel gāṛī "canceled" ho ga'ī hai.**
How long will it be delayed?	**Kitnī leṭ hai?**
There is a delay of . . . minutes.	**. . . minaṭ leṭ hai.**
There is a delay of . . . hours.	**. . . ghante leṭ hai.**
Excuse me, where is the ticket office?	**Māf kaṛye, ṭikiṭ-ghar kahāṅ hai?**

Where can I buy a ticket?	**Maiṅ ṭikiṭ kahāṅ se le saktā hūṅ?**
I want to go to . . .	**Maiṅ . . . jānā cāhtā hūṅ.**
I want a ticket to . . .	**Mujhe . . . kā ṭikiṭ cāhīye.**
I would like . . .	**Mujhe . . . cāhīye.**
a one-way ticket	**ek taraf kā ṭikiṭ**
a return ticket	**vāpsī kā ṭikiṭ**
first class	**pehle darje kā**
second class	**dūsre darje kā**
Do I pay in dollars?	**Maiṅ ḍālar meṅ paisā dūṅgā?**
You must pay in dollars.	**Ḍālar meṅ paisā dījye.**
Can I reserve a place?	**Maiṅ jagā buk kar saktā hūṅ?**
How long does the trip take?	**Pūre safar meṅ kitnā vaqt lage gā?**
Is it a direct route?	**Vo sīdhā rāsta hai?**

—By air

> All of Pakistan's international and national flights are non-smoking.

Is there a flight to . . . ?	**. . . ke līye havā'ī jahāz hai?**
When is the next flight to . . . ?	**. . . ke līye dūsrā havā'ī jahāz kab hai?**
How long is the flight?	**Havā'ī jahāz kā safar kitnā lambā hai?**
What is the flight number?	**Havā'ī jahāz kā namber kyā hai?**

a = apple. **ā** = father. **e** = pay. **i** = sit. **ī** = heat. **o** = hotel. **u** = put. **ū** = shoot. **au** = oar. **ai** = pay.

You must check in at . . .	**Āp ko . . . per caik-in karnā hogā.**
Is the flight delayed?	**Havā'ī-jahāz leṭ hai?**
How long is the flight delayed?	**Havā'ī-jahāz kitnā leṭ hai?**
Is this the flight for . . . ?	**kyā ye . . . kā havā'ī jahāz hai?**
When is the London flight arriving?	**London kā havā'ī-jahāz kab ā rahā hai?**
Is it on time?	**Kyā vo vaqt per hai?**
Is it late?	**Kyā vo laiṭ hai?**
Do I have to change planes?	**Mujha havā'ī jahāz badalnā ho gā?**
Has the plane left Dubai yet?	**Havā'ī-jahāz abhī Dubā'ī choṛ cukā hai?**
What time does the plane take off?	**Havā'ī-jahāz kab uṛe gā?**
What time do we arrive in Karachi?	**Ham Karacī kab poṅhceṅ ge?**
excess baggage	**ziyāda sāmān**
international flight	**ğair mulkī havā'ī safar**
internal/domestic flight	**andarūnī havā'ī safar**

—By bus

bus stop	**bas stap**
Where is the bus stop/station?	**Bas stap/isṭeshan kahāṅ hai?**
Take me to the bus station.	**Mujhe bas stap laijā'īye.**
Which bus goes to . . . ?	**Konsī bas . . . jātī hai?**
Does this bus go to . . . ?	**Kyā ye bas . . . jātī hai?**
How often do buses leave?	**Kitnī bar bas jātī hai?**

What time is the . . . bus?	**Kitne baje . . . bas hai?**
next	**aglī**
first	**pehlī**
last	**āxrī**
Will you let me know when we get to . . . ?	**Āp mujhe batā'aiṅ ge, ham . . . kab ā'eṅge?**
Stop, I want to get off!	**Rukye, maiṅ utarnā cāhtā hūṅ!**
Where can I get a bus to . . . ?	**. . . kī bas kahāṅ mile gī?**
When is the first bus to . . . ?	**. . . kī pehlī bas kab hai?**
When is the last bus to . . . ?	**. . . kī axrī bas kab hai?**
When is the next bus to . . . ?	**. . . kī aglī bas kab hai?**
Do I have to change buses?	**Mujhe bas badalnā hai?**
How long is the journey?	**Safar kitnā lambā hai?**
What is the fare?	**Kirāya kitnā hai?**
I want to get off at . . .	**Maiṅ . . . per utarnā cāhtā hūṅ.**
Please let me off at the next stop.	**Mujhe agale bas istāp per utāṛye.**
Please let me off here.	**Mujhe yahāṅ utārne dījye.**
I need my luggage, please.	**Mujhe merā sāmān cāhīye.**
That's my bag.	**Vo mera beg hai.**

—By rail

Passengers must . . .	**Musāfiroṅ ko . . . hai.**
change trains	**gaṛī badalnī**
change platforms	**plaitfārm badalnā**
Is this the right platform for . . . ?	**Kyā ye . . . ke līye sahī plaitfarm hai?**
The train leaves from platform . . .	**Gāṛī . . . se jātī hai.**
Take me to the railway station.	**Mujhe tren isṭeshan le jā'īye.**
Where can I buy tickets?	**Maiṅ ṭikiṭ kahāṅ xarīd saktā hūṅ?**
Which platform should I go to?	**Mujhe kon se plaitfarm per jāna hai?**
platform one/two	**plaitfarm ek/do**
You must change trains at . . .	**Āp ko . . . per train badalnā hai.**
Will the train leave on time?	**Gāṛī vaqt per hai?**
There will be a delay of . . . minutes.	**Vahāṅ per . . . minaṭ kī der hogī.**
There will be a delay of . . . hours.	**Vahāṅ per . . . ghante kī der hogī.**

—By taxi

Taxi!	**Taiksī!**
Where can I get a taxi?	**Mujhe taiksī kahāṅ milegī?**
Please could you get me a taxi.	**Mere līye taiksī lā'īye.**
Can you take me to . . . ?	**Āp mujhe . . . le jā sakte haiṅ?**

How much will it cost to . . . ?	**. . . ke līye kitnā paisā hogā?**
To this address, please.	**Is pate per.**
Turn left.	**Bā'aiṅ muṛye.**
Turn right.	**Dā'aiṅ muṛye.**
Go straight ahead.	**Sīdhe jā'īye.**
The next corner, please.	**Agle moṛ per.**
The next street to the left.	**Aglī saṛak per bāyāṅ.**
The next street to the right.	**Aglī saṛak per dāyāṅ.**
Stop!	**Rukye!**
Don't stop!	**Mat rukye!**
I'm in a hurry.	**Maiṅ jaldī meṅ hūṅ.**
Please drive slowly!	**Dhīre calā'īye!**
Stop here!	**Yahāṅ rukye!**
Stop the car, I want to get out.	**Gāṛī rokye maiṅ utarnā cāhtā hūṅ.**
Please wait here.	**Yehāṅ intizār kījye.**

—General phrases

I want to get off at . . .	**Maiṅ . . . per utarnā cāhtā hūṅ.**
Excuse me!	**Māf kaṛye!**
Excuse me, may I get by?	**Māf kaṛye, āge jā saktā hūṅ?**
These are my bags.	**Ye mere beg haiṅ.**
Please put them there.	**Us ko idhar rakh dījye.**
Is this seat free?	**Kyā ye sīṭ xālī hai?**
I think that's my seat.	**Mere xiyāl se ye merī sīṭ hai.**

a = apple. **ā** = father. **e** = pay. **i** = sit. **ī** = heat. **o** = hotel. **u** = put. **ū** = shoot. **au** = oar. **ai** = pay.

—Travel words

airport	**havā'ī-adda**
airport tax	**"airport tax"**
ambulance	**"ambulance"**
arrivals	**āmad/āne vāla hisā**
baggage counter	**samman kī khiṛkī**
bicycle	**sā'ikal**
boarding pass	**"boarding pass"**
boat	**kashtī**
bus stop	**bas-stop**
car	**gāṛī**
check-in counter	**"check-in counter"**
closed	**band**
customs	**"customs"**
delay	**der**
departures	**rawānagī**
dining car	**"dining car"**
emergency exit	**"emergency exit"**
entrance	**dāxlā**
exit	**bāhar jane kā rāsta**
express	**taiz** *or* **jaldī se**
ferry	**"ferry"**
4-wheel drive	**"4-wheel drive"**
information	**mālūmāt**
ladies/gents	**aurteṅ/mard**
local	**desī**
helicopter	**"helicopter"**
horse and cart	**ghoṛe kī baghī**
motorbike	**motar-sā'ikil**
no entry	**rāsta band**
no smoking	**sigret pīna manā hai**
open	**khulā**
platform number	**plaitfārm kā nambar**
railway	**"railway"**
reserved	**"reserved"**

road	**saṛak**
sign	**nishān**
sleeping car	**"sleeping car"**
station	**isṭeshan**
subway	**"subway"**
ticket office	**ṭikiṭ ghar**
timetable	**tā'iming** *or* **auqāt**
toilet(s)	**bait-ul-xalā** *or* **pāxāna**
town center	**shehar kā markaz**
train station	**tren isṭeshan**

—Disabilities

wheelchair	**"wheelchair"**
disabled	**māzūr** *or* **maflūj**
Do you have seats for the disabled?	**Āp ke pās mazūr logoṅ ke līye sīṭ hai?**
Do you have access for the disabled?	**Āp ke pās mazūr logoṅ ke līye rāsta hai?**
Do you have facilities for the disabled?	**Āp ke pās mazūr logoṅ ke līye intizām hai?**

a = *apple*. **ā** = *father*. **e** = *pay*. **i** = *sit*. **ī** = *heat*. **o** = *hotel*. **u** = *put*. **ū** = *shoot*. **au** = *oar*. **ai** = *pay*.

7. ACCOMMODATION

Pakistan offers a wide range of hotels from familiar five-star international chains to humble budget establishments. In addition to providing all mod-cons, good hotels can often be the perfect place to familiarize yourself with the local cuisine or find alternative western dishes, since many have excellent restaurants that can cater to all tastes.

I am looking for a . . .	**Maiṅ . . . dhūnḍ rahā hūṅ.**
guesthouse	**"guesthouse"**
hotel	**hoṭal**
hostel	**"hostel"**
Is there anywhere to stay for the night?	**Yehāṅ ko'ī jagā hai jahāṅ maiṅ rāt ko ṭhair saktā hūṅ?**
Where is a . . . hotel?	**. . . hoṭal kahāṅ hai?**
cheap	**sastā**
good	**achchā**
nearby	**qarībī**
What is the address?	**Patā kyā hai?**
Could you write the address please?	**Patā likhye?**

—At the hotel

Do you have any rooms free?	**Ko'ī kamrā xāli hai?**
I would like . . .	**Mujhe . . . cāhīye.**
a single room	**chotā kamra**
a double room	**baṛā kamra**
We'd like a room.	**Hamaiṅ kamra cāhīye.**
We'd like two rooms.	**Hamaiṅ do kamre cāhī'yaiṅ.**

c = *church.* **ṅ** = *sing.* **x** = *loch.* **ğ/q** *see p18.* **bh/ch/dh/ḍh/gh/kh/ph/ṛh/th/ṭh** = *breathed.* **ḍ/ṛ/ṭ** = *flapped.*

I want a room with . . .	**Mujhe aik . . . vāla kamra cāhīye.**
a bathroom	**ğusal-xāna**
a shower	**shāvar**
a television	**TV**
a window	**khiṛkī**
a double bed	**dabal beḍ**
a balcony	**bālkanī**
a view	**nazāra**
I want a room that's quiet.	**Mujhe sukūn vāla kamra cāhīye.**
How long will you be staying?	**Āp kitne din ṭhairaiṅ ge?**
How many nights?	**Kitnī rātaiṅ?**
I'm going to stay for . . .	**Maiṅ . . . ṭhairūṅgā.**
one day	**ek din**
two days	**do din**
one week	**ek hafta**
Do you have any I.D.?	**Āp ke pās shanaxtī karḍ hai?**
Sorry, we're full.	**Māf kaṛye, ye "full" hai.**
I have a reservation.	**Merā rezerveshan hai.**
I have to meet someone here.	**Mujhe yahāṅ kisī se milnā hai.**
My name is . . .	**Merā nām . . . hai.**
May I speak to the manager please?	**Maiṅ "manager" se bāt kar saktā hūṅ?**
How much is it per night?	**Ek rāt ke līye kitnā hai?**
How much is it per person?	**Ek ādmī ke līye kitnā hai?**
How much is it per week?	**Ek hafta kā kitnā?**
It's . . . per night.	**Ek rāt kā . . . hai.**

It's . . . per person.	**Ek ādmī kā . . . hai.**
It's . . . per week.	**Ek hafta kā . . . hai.**
Can I see it?	**Maiṅ dekh sakta hūṅ?**
Are there any others?	**Dūsre log bhī haiṅ?**
Is there . . . ?	**Yahāṅ per . . . hai?**
air-conditioning	**"air-conditioning"**
a telephone	**talifon**
a bar	**"bar"**
hot water	**garam pānī**
laundry service	**laundrī kī sahūlat**
room service	**kamre kī sarvis**
No, I don't like it.	**Mujhe ye pasand nahīṅ.**
Its too . . .	**Ye bohut . . . hai.**
cold	**ṭhanḍa**
hot	**garam**
big	**baṛā**
dark	**tārīk**
small	**chotā**
noisy	**shor-pukār vāla**
dirty	**gandā**
Its fine, I'll take it.	**Ye ṭhīk hai, maiṅ le lūṅ gā.**
Where is the bathroom?	**Ğusal-xāna?**
Is there hot water all day?	**Yahāṅ din-bhar garam panī hai?**
Do you have a safe?	**Āp ke pās mehfūz lākar hai?**
Is there anywhere to wash clothes?	**Yehāṅ kapṛe dhone kī jaga hai?**
Can I use the telephone?	**Maiṅ fon istimāl kar saktā hūṅ?**

c = *church*. **ṅ** = *sing*. **x** = lo*ch*. **ğ/q** *see p18*. **bh/ch/dh/ḍh/gh/kh/ph/ṛh/th/ṭh** = *breathed*. **ḍ/ṛ/ṭ** = *flapped*.

—Needs

I need . . .	**Mujhe . . . cāhīye.**
candles	**mom-battī**
toilet paper	**"toilet paper"**
soap	**sābun**
clean sheets	**na'ī cādar**
an extra blanket	**ek aur "blanket"**
drinking water	**pīne kā pānī**
a light bulb	**"light bulb"**
a mosquito net	**machchar dānī**
mosquito repellent	**machchar bhagāne kī davā**
Please change the sheets.	**Cādar badalye.**
Can I have the key to my room?	**Mujhe mere kamre kī cābī cāhīye.**
I can't close . . .	**Maiṅ . . . band nahīn kar saktā.**
I can't open	**Maiṅ . . . khol nahīn saktā.**
the window	**khiṛkī**
the door	**darvāza**
I have lost my key.	**Merī cābī gum gā'ī hai.**
The shower won't work.	**Shāvar kām nahīṅ kartā.**
How do I get hot water?	**Garam panī kaise ātā hai?**
The toilet won't flush.	**Falesh kām nahīṅ kartā.**
The water has been cut off.	**Pānī kī lā'in kaṭ gā'ī hai.**
The electricity has been cut off.	**Bijlī kaṭ gā'ī hai.**
The gas has been cut off.	**Gais kat gā'ī hai.**

a = apple. **ā** = father. **e** = pay. **i** = sit. **ī** = heat. **o** = hotel. **u** = put. **ū** = shoot. **au** = oar. **ai** = pay.

The air-conditioning doesn't work.	**"Air-condition" kām nahīṅ kartā.**
The phone doesn't work.	**Fon kām nahīṅ kartā.**
I can't flush the toilet.	**Maiṅ falash nahīn kar saktā.**
The toilet is blocked.	**"Toilet" blāk hai.**
I can't switch off the tap.	**Maiṅ toṅtī band nahī kar saktā.**
I need a plug for the bath.	**Mujhe tab ke līye palag cāhīye.**
Where is the plug socket?	**Palag kā sākiṭ kahāṅ hai?**
There are strange insects in my room.	**Mere kamre meṅ ajīb-o-ğarīb kīṛe haiṅ.**
There's an animal in my room.	**Mere kamre meṅ ek jānvar hai.**
wake-up call	**uṭhāne ke līye**
Could you wake me up at . . . o'clock?	**Āp mujhe . . . baje uṭhā'īye?**
I am leaving now.	**Maiṅ ab jā rahā hūṅ.**
We are leaving now.	**Ham ab jā rahe haiṅ.**
May I pay the bill now?	**Maiṅ abb bil de dūṅ.**

—Useful words

bathroom	**ğusal-xāna**
bed	**bistar**
blanket	**"blanket"**
candle	**mom-battī**
chair	**kursī**
cold water	**ṭhandā pānī**
cupboard	**almārī**
door lock	**darvāze kā tāla**
electricity	**bijlī**

c = *church.* **ṅ** = *sing.* **x** = *loch.* **ğ/q** *see p18.* **bh/ch/dh/ḍh/gh/kh/ph/ṛh/th/ṭh** = *breathed.* **ḍ/ṛ/ṭ** = *flapped.*

excluded	**ke binā**
extra	**zā'id**
fridge	**"fridge"**
hot water	**garam pānī**
included	**shāmil**
key	**cābī**
laundry	**lāndrī**
mattress	**gadda**
meals	**khāne**
mirror	**ā'īnā**
name	**nām**
noise	**shor**
padlock	**zanjīr vāla tāla**
pillow	**takyā**
plug (electric)	**palag**
quiet	**xāmūsh**
room	**kamra**
room number	**kamare kā nambar**
sheet	**cādar**
shower	**shāvar**
suitcase	**"suitcase"**
surname	**xāndānī nām**
table	**mez**
towel	**tolīya**
water	**pānī**
window	**khiṛkī**

LAUNDRY — Hotels will be able to arrange for your laundry to be done, but if you need to do your own you can easily find good detergents in local markets.

a = apple. **ā** = father. **e** = pay. **i** = sit. **ī** = heat. **o** = hotel. **u** = put. **ū** = shoot. **au** = oar. **ai** = pay.

8. FOOD & DRINK

Apart from traditional Pakistani food, the major cities have a good selection of restaurants serving international dishes including Italian, Chinese, Japanese, Thai, and Persian as well as popular U.S. and continental dishes. In the citiy centers you'll easily spot outlets of well-known international chains offering pizzas and hamburgers. Many good hotels also have excellent restaurants serving sumptuous meals, but don't let that stop you from venturing out to explore some of the many fine local restaurants.

breakfast	**nāshtā**
lunch	**dopehar kā khāna**
snack	**halka-phulka khāna**
dinner/supper	**shām kā khāna**
dessert	**mīṭhā**

MEALS — Pakistanis do not use separate names for meals as in English. Some of the terms given above are rather literal, and lunch and dinner/supper are usually just called **khānā** "meal." Cooked dishes are called **masnū'āt**.

I'm hungry.	**Maiṅ bhūkā hūṅ.**
I'm thirsty.	**Maiṅ piyāsa hūṅ.**
Do you know a good restaurant?	**Āp ko achcha raistoranṭ patā hai?**
Do you have a table, please?	**Āp ke pās xālī tebal hai?**
I would like a table for . . . people, please.	**Mujhe . . . logoṅ ke līye ṭebal cāhīye.**
Can I see the menu please?	**Maiṅ menyū dekh saktā hūṅ?**
I'm still looking at the menu.	**Maiṅ abhī menyū dekh rahā hūṅ.**
I would like to order now.	**Maiṅ ādar karnā cāhtā hūṅ.**

c = *church.* **ṅ** = *sing.* **x** = *loch.* **ğ/q** *see p18.* **bh/ch/dh/ḍh/gh/kh/ph/ṛh/th/ṭh** = *breathed.* **ḍ/ṛ/ṭ** = *flapped.*

What's this?	**Ye kyā hai?**
Is it spicy?	**Ye masale-dār hai?**
Does it have meat in it?	**Kyā is meṅ gosht hai?**
There is no meat in it.	**Is meṅ gosht nahīṅ hai.**
Does it have alcohol in it?	**Kyā is meṅ alkohal hai?**
Do you have . . . ?	**Āp ke pās . . . hai?**
We don't have . . .	**Hamāre pās . . . nahīṅ hai.**
Do you want . . . ?	**Āp ko . . . cāhīye?**
Can I order some more . . . ?	**. . . maiṅ aur āḍar kar saktā hūṅ?**
That's all, thank you.	**Bas, shukriyā.**
That's enough, thanks.	**Ye kāfī hai, shukriya.**
I am still eating.	**Maiṅ khā rahā hūṅ.**
I have finished eating.	**Maiṅ khā cukā hūṅ.**
I am full up!	**Merā paiṭ bhar geā hai!**
I am a vegetarian.	**Maiṅ sabzī xor hūṅ.**
I don't eat meat.	**Maiṅ gosht nahīṅ khāta.**
I don't eat pork.	**Maiṅ sūvar kā gosht nahīṅ khāta.**
I don't eat chicken or fish.	**Maiṅ murğī yā machlī nahīṅ khāta.**
I don't drink alcohol.	**Maiṅ alkohal/sharāb nahīṅ pītā.**

—Needs

I would like . . .	**Mujhe . . . cāhīye.**
an ashtray	**"ashtray"**
the bill	**bil** *or* **hisāb**
the menu	**menyū**
a glass of water	**pānī kā gilās**

a = apple. **ā** = father. **e** = pay. **i** = sit. **ī** = heat. **o** = hotel. **u** = put. **ū** = shoot. **au** = oar. **ai** = pay.

a bottle of water	**pānī kī botal**
a bottle of wine	**sharāb kī botal**
a bottle of beer	**"beer" kī botal**
another bottle (of . . .)	**(kī . . .) dosrī boṭal**
a bottle-opener	**boṭal kholne kī cābī**
dessert	**mīṭhā**
a drink	**sharbat**
a fork	**kāṭa**
another chair	**dūsrī kursī**
another plate	**dūsrī jagā**
another glass	**dūsrā gilās**
another cup	**dūsrā kap**
a napkin	**dūsrī dastī** *or* **naipkin**
a glass	**ek gilās**
a knife	**ek cāqū**
a plate	**ek pilaiṭ**
a spoon	**ek camac**
a table	**ek tebal**
a teaspoon	**ek cā'ai kā camac**
a toothpick	**ek xilāl**

too much	**bohut ziyāda**
too little	**bohut kam**
not enough	**kāfī nahīṅ**

—Tastes

fresh fruit	**tāze phal**
fresh fish	**tāzī machlī**
spicy (hot)	**masāle dār**
stale	**bāsī**
sour	**kaṛvā**
sweet	**mīṭhā**
bitter	**talx** *or* **khatta**
hot	**garam**
cold	**ṭhanḍā**
salty	**namkīn**

c = *church.* **ṅ** = si*ng.* **x** = lo*ch.* **ğ/q** *see p18.* **bh/ch/dh/ḍh/gh/kh/ph/ṛh/th/ṭh** = *breathed.* **ḍ/ṛ/ṭ** = *flapped.*

tasteless	**be-mazā**
bad	**burā**
tasty	**lazīz**

—Food

bread *regular*	**roṭī**
flat	**nān**
candy	**miṭhā'i; shīrīni**
cheese	**panīr** *or* **cīz**
chewing gum	**ching-gam**
chutney	**caṭnī**
egg	**anḍā**
flour	**āṭā**
french fries	**ālū ke cips**
ghee	**ghī**
honey	**shaihid**
ice-cream	**āis-krīm**
mustard	**rā'ī**
oil	**tel**
pasta	**pastā**
pepper	**kālī mirc**
rice	**cāval**
salad	**salād**
salt	**namak**
sandwich	**"sandwich"**
soup	**sūp**
spices	**masala**
sugar	**shakar** *or* **cīnī**
sweets	**miṭhā'i; shīrīni**
vinegar	**sirkā**
yogurt	**dahī**

> **RICE** — **Cāval** is uncooked rice. Cooked rice in Pakistani cuisine becomes pilau (**pulao**) or some other term depending on the dish, such as **biryānī**. It's not eaten as plain white rice.

—Vegetables & fruit

apple	**seb**
beans	**bīj** *or* **phallī**
cauliflower	**gobhī**
chickpeas	**chana**
cucumber	**khairā**
grape	**angūr**
lemon; lime	**līmo**
lentils	**dāl**
mango	**ām**
melon	**xarbūz**
nut: almond	**badam**
pistacchio	**pista**
walnut	**akhrot**
okra	**bhindi**
orange	**santarā**
peach	**ārū**
peas	**maṭar**
pineapple	**anānās**
plum	**alūcha; zard ālu**
potato	**ālū**
sweet potato	**shakar qaṅd**
pumpkin	**kaddū**
spinach	**sāg**
tomato	**ṭamāṭar**
vegetables	**sabzī** *or* **tarkārī**
watermelon	**tarbūz**

—Meat & fish

beef	**gā'e kā gosht**
chicken	**murğī kā gosht**
fish	**machlī**
kebab	**kabāb**
lamb	**bheṛ**
meat	**gosht**

c = *church*. **ṅ** = *sing*. **x** = *loch*. **ğ/q** *see p18*. **bh/ch/dh/ḍh/gh/kh/ph/ṛh/th/ṭh** = *breathed*. **ḍ/ṛ/ṭ** = *flapped*.

—Drinks

ALCOHOL — Muslims are prohibited from drinking alcohol in Pakistan. However, as a foreigner you will be able to enjoy a drink at good hotels or at one of a number of state approved bars. In addition to imported alcohol you will also find locally brewed beers and spirits. Don't attempt to bring alcoholic drink into the country because it's illegal.

alcohol	**sharāb**
beer	**"beer"**
bottle	**botal**
can	**kan** *or* **ḍabā**
coffee	**kāfī**
coffee with milk	**dūdh kī kāfī**
fruit juice	**phal kā jūs** *or* **arq**
ice	**baraf**
milk	**dūdh**
mineral water	**ma'daniyātī pānī**
tea	**cā'e**
tea with lemon	**nībū kī cā'e**
tea with milk	**dūdh kī cā'e**
no sugar, please	**binā shakar ke**

More on food . . .

Pakistani cuisine draws on a long and rich tradition. Main dishes are served with rice and a number of baked and fried breads such as chapatis and nan. Meat may be roasted (**bhūnā**) or cooked in a traditional clay oven (**tandūrī**). Some of the more popular main dishes are: **sīkh kebabs** – made from minced meat that is rolled up, placed on skewers and cooked over a charcoal fire; and **shami kebabs** – round flat patties made from a mixture of minced meat, **dāl** (lentils) and special spices which are then fried in oil. **Koftas** are meatballs that are served up in a spicy sauce. Chicken dishes include **korma** (a mild and creamy curry dish), **nihari**, **tikka**, **karahi** and **shashlik**. To round off the meal, try the local ice-cream varieties of **kulfi**, **firni** and **khīr**. Finish off your meal with fruit (**phal**), washed down with the ubiquitous tea or bottled drinks.

9. DIRECTIONS

Where is . . . ?	**. . . kahāṅ hai?**
the academy	**"academy"**
the airport	**havā'ī aḍḍa**
the art gallery	**"art gallery"**
a bank	**"bank"**
the cathedral	**baṛā girjā**
the church	**girjā ghar**
the city center	**shehar kā markaz**
the consulate/embassy	**sifārat xāna**
the . . . embassy	**. . . sifārat xāna**
my hotel	**merā hoṭal**
the information office	**"information" kā āfis**
the internet café	**"internet café"**
the main square	**baṛa chorāha**
the market	**bazār**
the monastery	**"monastery"**
the mosque	**masjid**
the museum	**ajā'ib-ghar**
parliament	**"parliament"**
the police station	**polīs isṭeshan**
the post office	**ḍāk xāna**
the station	**isṭeshan**
the telephone center	**"telephone center"**
a toilet	**bait-ul-xalā** *or* **pāxāna**
the university	**"university"**

Which . . . is this?	**Ye konsā . . . hai?**
bridge	**pul**
building	**imārat**
district	**qasbā**
river	**nadī**

c = *church.* **ṅ** = *sing.* **x** = *loch.* **ğ/q** *see p18.* **bh/ch/dh/ḍh/gh/kh/ph/ṛh/th/ṭh** = *breathed.* **ḍ/ṛ/ṭ** = *flapped.*

road	**saṛak**
street	**saṛak**
suburb	**muzāfāt**
village	**gā'on**
What is this building?	**Ye bilḍing kyā hai?**
What is that building?	**Vo bilḍing kyā hai?**
What time does it open?	**Vo kis vaqt khultā hai?**
What time does it close?	**Vo kis vaqt band hotā hai?**
Are we on the right road for . . . ?	**Kyā ham . . . ke sahī rāste per haiṅ?**
How many kilometers is it to . . . ?	**. . . kitne kilomīṭar dūr hai?**
It is . . . kilometers away.	**Vo . . . kilomīṭar dūr hai.**
How far is the next village?	**Aglā gā'on kitnī dūr hai?**
Where can I find this address?	**Mujhe ye patā kahāṅ mile gā?**
Can you show me on the map?	**Āp naqshā dikhā sakte haiṅ?**
How do I get to . . . ?	**Maiṅ . . . kaise jā saktā hūṅ?**
I want to go to . . .	**Maiṅ . . . jānā cāhtā hūṅ.**
Can I walk there?	**Maiṅ vahāṅ paidal jā saktā hūṅ?**
Can I park here?	**Maiṅ yehāṅ gāṛī khaṛī kar saktā hūṅ?**

a = apple. **ā** = father. **e** = pay. **i** = sit. **ī** = heat. **o** = hotel. **u** = put. **ū** = shoot. **au** = oar. **ai** = pay.

Is it far?	**Kyā vo dūr hai?**
Is it near?	**Kyā vo qarīb hai?**
Is it far from/near here?	**Kyā vo yahāṅ se qarīb/dūr hai?**
It is not far.	**Kyā vo dūr nahīṅ hai.**
Go straight ahead.	**Sīdhe jā'īye.**
Turn left.	**Bā'aiṅ muṛye.**
Turn right.	**Dā'aiṅ muṛye.**
at the next corner	**agle moṛ per**
at the traffic lights	**aglī traifik kī lā'it per**

—Directions

behind	**pīche**
far	**dūr**
in front of	**ke sāmne**
left	**bāyāṅ**
left: on the left	**bāyāṅ hāth par**
near	**qarīb**
opposite	**āmne-sāmne**
right	**dāyāṅ**
right: on the right	**dāyāṅ hāth par**
straight on	**sīdhe**
corner	**moṛ**
crossroads	**corāha**
one-way street	**ek taraf saṛak**
north	**shimāl**
south	**junūb**
east	**mashriq**
west	**mağrib**

10. SHOPPING

The shops and markets of Pakistan's cities and towns are overflowing with wonderful things to buy. The Anarkali Bazaar in Lahore sells traditional crafts such as leatherwear, gold and silver jewellery, silk articles and embroidered garments. Karachi's Zainab Market is also noted for its leather goods and the city is the perfect place to pick up a fine Pakistani, Iranian or Afghan carpet or rug.

HAGGLING — Don't expect to find fixed prices in Pakistan's bazaars and don't be fazed if quoted a princely sum for an object you've taken a shine to. This is an invitation to bargain. Politely offer a lower price that you think is a fairer price, and soon both you and the seller should come to a happy compromise.

Where can I find a . . . ?	**. . . kahāṅ miltā hai?**
Where can I buy . . . ?	**. . . kahāṅ xarīd saktā hūṅ?**
Where is the market?	**Bāzār kahāṅ hai?**
Where is the nearest . . . ?	**Sab se qarīb . . . kahāṅ hai?**
Can you help me?	**Āp merī madad kar sakte haiṅ?**
Can I help you?	**Maiṅ āp kī madad kar saktā hūṅ?**
I'm just looking.	**Maiṅ sirf dekh rahā hūṅ.**
I'd like to buy . . .	**Maiṅ xarīdenā cāhūṅ gā . . .**
Could you show me some . . . ?	**Āp mujhe dikhā sakte haiṅ kuch . . . ?**
Can I look at it?	**Maiṅ ise dekh saktā hūṅ?**
Do you have any . . . ?	**Āp ke pās ko'ī . . . hai?**

a = apple. **ā** = father. **e** = pay. **i** = sit. **ī** = heat. **o** = hotel. **u** = put. **ū** = shoot. **au** = oar. **ai** = pay.

This.	**Ye.**
That.	**Vo.**
I don't like it.	**Mujhe ye pasand nahīṅ.**
I like it.	**Mujhe ye pasand hai.**
cheaper	**sastā**
better	**achchā**
Do you have anything else?	**Āp ke pās kuch aur hai?**
Sorry, this is the only one.	**Māf kaṛye, ye sirf ek hai.**
I'll take it.	**Maiṅ ise lūṅgā.**
How much/many do you want?	**Kitne cāhīye?**
How much is it?	**Ye kitne kā hai?**
Can you write down the price?	**Āp qīmat likh sakte haiṅ?**
Can you lower the price?	**Āp qīmat kam kaṛye?**
I don't have much money.	**Mere pās bohut paisā nahīṅ.**
Do you take credit cards?	**Āp ke pās "credit card" hai?**
Will that be all?	**Bas itnā hogā?**
Thank you, goodbye.	**Shukriyā, xudā hāfiz.**
I want to return this.	**Maiṅ ise vāpas karnā cāhtā hūṅ.**

—Outlets

baker's	**bekrī**
bank	**bank**
barber	**hajjam**
I'd like a haircut.	**Mujhe bāl katvānā hai.**
bookshop	**kitāb kī dūkān**

butcher's	**qasā'ī kī dūkān**
chemist's	**davā'ī kī dūkān**
clothes shop	**kapṛe kī dūkān**
dentist	**dāṅt kā ḍaktar**
department store	**"department store"**
dressmaker	**darzī**
electrical goods store	**biglī ke sāmān kī dūkān**
greengrocer	**sabzī vāla**
hairdresser	**hajam** *or* **nā'ī**
hardware store	**"hardware" kī dūkān**
hospital	**haspatāl**
laundry	**laundrī** *or* **dhobī kī dūkān**
market	**bāzār**
shoe shop	**jūte kī dūkān**
shop	**dūkān**
stationer's	**isṭeshnarī**
supermarket	**baṛā mārkiṭ** *or* **"supermarket"**
travel agent	**"travel agent"**
vegetable shop	**sabzī kī dūkān**
watchmaker's	**ghaṛī sāz**

—Gifts

box	**ḍabba**
bracelet	**kaṛā**
candlestick	**mom battī**
carpet	**qālīn**
chain	**zanjīr**
clock	**ghaṛī**
copper	**tāṅba**
crystal	**"crystal"**
earrings	**bude** *or* **jhumke**
enamel	**"enamel"**

a = apple. **ā** = father. **e** = pay. **i** = sit. **ī** = heat. **o** = hotel. **u** = put. **ū** = shoot. **au** = oar. **ai** = pay.

gold	**sonā**
handicraft	**dastī masno'āt**
iron	**lohā**
jewellery	**zevar**
leather	**camṛā**
metal	**dhāt**
modern	**jadīd**
necklace	**neklas** *or* **gale kā hār**
pottery	**cīnī ke bartan**
ring	**aṅgūṭī**
rosary	**tasbīh**
silver	**cāndī**
steel	**folād**
stone	**path-thar**
traditional	**rivāyatī**
watch	**ghaṛī**
wood	**lakṛī**

—Clothes

See "More on Clothing" on page 145.

bag	**beg**
belt	**"belt"** *or* **paṭā**
boots	**baṛe jūte**
cotton	**rū'ī** *or* **kapās**
dress	**libās**
gloves	**dastane**
handbag	**handbeg**
hat	**hat**
jacket	**"jacket"** *or* **sadrī**
jeans	**jīnz**
leather	**camṛa**
necktie	**tā'ī**
overcoat	**"overcoat"**
pocket	**jeb**

scarf	**dupaṭa**
shirt	**qamīs**
shoes	**jūte**
socks	**moze**
suit	**sūṭ**
sweater	**siweṭar**
tights	**tāyits**
trousers	**patlūn**
umbrella	**chatrī**
underwear	**"underwear"** *or* **jāṅgiā**
uniform	**"uniform"** *or* **vardī**
wool	**ūn**

—Toiletries

aspirin	**"aspirin"**
comb	**kanghā**
condom	**"condom"**
cotton wool	**rū'ī**
deodorant	**"deodorant"**
hairbrush	**bāl kā barash**
insect repellant	**machchar bhagāne kī davā**
lipstick	**"lipstick"**
mascara	**kājal**
mouthwash	**"mouthwash"**
nail-clippers	**nail-kāṭar**
perfume	**itar** *or* **"scent"**
plaster	**pilāstar**
powder	**"powder"**
razor	**"razor"**
razorblade	**"razorblade"**
safety pin	**hifāzatī pin**
sanitary towels	**"sanitary towels"**
shampoo	**shampū**

shaving cream	**"shaving cream"**
sleeping pills	**sone kī golī**
soap	**sābun**
sponge	**ispanj**
sunblock cream	**"suncream"** *or* **dhūp kā kirīm**
tampons	**"tampons"**
tissues	**"tissues"**
toilet paper	**"toilet paper"**
toothbrush	**dāṅt kā barash**
toothpaste	**dāṅt kā manjan**
washing powder	**dhone kā pā'odar**

—Stationery

ballpoint	**"ballpoint"**
book	**kitāb**
dictionary	**"dictionary"** *or* **luğat**
envelope	**lifā-fā**
guidebook	**"guidebook"**
ink	**siyāhī**
magazine	**parcā**
map	**naqshā**
a map of Lahore	**Lahore kā naqshā**
road map	**"road map"** *or* **saṛak kā naqshā**
newspaper	**axbār**
newspaper in English	**Angrezī axbār**
notebook	**"notebook"**
novel	**nāvil**
novels in English	**angraizī nāvil**
(piece of) paper	**kāğaz kā ṭukṛā**
pen	**qalam**
pencil	**"pencil"**
postcard	**"postcard"**
scissors	**qaiṅcī**

c = *church.* **ṅ** = *sing.* **x** = *loch.* **ğ/q** *see p18.* **bh/ch/dh/ḍh/gh/kh/ph/ṛh/th/ṭh** = *breathed.* **ḍ/ṛ/ṭ** = *flapped.*

—Photography

How much is it to process this film?	**Is film ko foto banāne kā kitnā hogā?**
When will it be ready?	**Kab tāyār hogī?**
I'd like film for this camera.	**Is kaimre ke līye film cāhīye.**
B&W (film)	**"black and white"**
camera	**kaimra**
colour (film)	**rangīn**
flash	**"flash"**
lens	**"lens"**
light meter	**"light" kā mīṭar**

—Electrical equipment

adapter	**palag kā aḍāpṭar**
battery	**"battery"**
cassette	**kaisit**
CD	**CD**
CD player	**CD pleyer**
fan	**paṅkhā**
hairdryer	**bāl sūkhāny kā paṅkhā**
iron (for clothing)	**istarī**
kettle	**ketlī**
plug	**palag**
portable T.V.	**"portable T.V."**
radio	**radio**
record	**"record"**
tape (cassette)	**taip**
tape-recorder	**taip-rekorder**
television	**"television"**
transformer	**"transformer"**
video-player	**video-pleyer**

a = apple. **ā** = father. **e** = pay. **i** = s*i*t. **ī** = heat. **o** = h*o*tel. **u** = p*u*t. **ū** = sh*oo*t. **au** = *oa*r. **ai** = pay.

videotape	**videotaip**
voltage regulator	**"voltage regulator"**

LANGUAGE TIP — For hi-tech items like cassettes, videos, CDs, DVDs, video-players, or transformers you are more likely to be understood if you use the English terms.

—Sizes

small	**chotā**
big	**baṛā**
heavy	**vaznī**
light	**halkā**
more	**aur**
less	**kam**
many	**kā'ī**
too much/too many	**bohut sare**
enough	**kāfī**
that's enough	**ye kāfī hai**
also	**bhī**
a little bit	**thoṛa sā**
I'd like a carrier bag to carry these things in.	**Mujhe ye cīzaiṅ le jāni ko beg cāhīye.**

—Colors

black	**kāla**
pink	**gulābī**
blue	**nīlā**
purple	**baiṅgnī**
brown	**bhūrā**
red	**lāl**
green	**harā**
white	**safaid**
orange	**nārangī**
yellow	**pīlā**

11. WHAT'S TO SEE

Pakistan has many superb examples of Islamic architecture including mosques and palaces, as well as Buddhist monuments and Hindu temples. The country also has a number of fascinating museums including those of Lahore, Peshawar and Islamabad as well as the National Museum in Karachi. These offer a wonderful glimpse into the cultures that have inhabited the region since time immemorial. Exhibitions include the art and culture of the ancient Indus Valley, fine collections covering the Moghal Empire, Sikh woodwork and lots of exhibits on Buddhism.

NATURE — Pakistan has a number of national parks which, in addition to their stunning landscapes and settings, offer a good opportunity to see some of the country's richly varied wildlife. Finding a guide who knows the park well is indispensable. Some of Pakistan's wildlife include leopards, black bears, the red flying squirrel, rhesus macaques, barking deer, jackals and foxes as well as a multitude of reptiles. The very lucky might spot a snow leopard. Bird lovers will find a paradise of creatures to watch including many birds of prey such as golden eagles, griffin vultures, peregrine falcons and kestrels.

Do you have a guidebook?	**Āp ke pās gā'iḍ buk hai?**
Do you have a local map?	**Āp ke pās is ilaqe kā naqsha hai?**
Is there a guide who speaks English?	**Yahāṅ kū'ī gā'iḍ Angrezī bolatā hai?**
What are the main attractions?	**Dekhne kī cīzāiṅ kyā haiṅ?**
What is that?	**Vo kyā hai?**
How old is it?	**Vo kitnā purāna hai?**
What animal is that?	**Vo kon sā jānvar hai?**
What fish is that?	**Vo kon sī machlī hai?**
What insect is that?	**Vo kon sā kīṛa hai?**

a = apple. **ā** = father. **e** = pay. **i** = sit. **ī** = heat. **o** = hotel. **u** = put. **ū** = shoot. **au** = oar. **ai** = pay.

May I take a photograph?	**Maiṅ foto le saktā hūṅ?**
What time does it open?	**Ye kitne baje khultā hai?**
What time does it close?	**Ye kitne baje band hotā hai?**
What does that say?	**Vo kyā likhā hai?**
Who is that statue of?	**Vo mujasama kyā hai?**
Is there an entrance fee?	**Kyā yahāṅ dāxle kī fīs hai?**
How much?	**Kitnī hai?**
Are there any night-clubs/discos?	**Kyā yahāṅ nā'iṭ-kalab/ disko haiṅ?**
How much does it cost to get in?	**Andar jāni kā kitnā paisa hai?**
When is the wedding?	**Shadī kab hai?**
What time does it begin?	**Ye kitne baje shurū hotā hai?**
Can we swim here?	**Kiā ham vahāṅ tair sakte haiṅ?**

—Activities

dancing	**nacnā**
disco	**disko**
exhibition	**numā'ish**
folk dancing	**desī nāc**
folk music	**desī mosīqī**
jazz	**"jazz"**
nightclub	**nā'iṭ-kalab**
party	**"party"**
pop music	**"pop music"**
pub	**"pub"**

—Places

apartment	"apartment" *or* flaiṭ
archaeological	āsār-e-qadīma
art gallery	"art gallery"
bakery	"bakery"
bar	bar
apartment block	"apartment" vālī imārat
building	imārat
casino	"casino"
castle	qila
cemetery	qabarastān
church	"church"
cinema	"cinema"
city map	shehar kā naqaha
college	"college"
concert hall	"concert hall"
concert	"concert"
embassy	sifārat xāna
fort	qilā
hospital	aspatāl
house	makān
industrial estate	inḍastrī kā ilāqa
library	"library"
main square	baṛa corāha
market	bāzār
monument	yadgār
mosque	masjid
museum	ajā'ib ghar
old city	purāna shehar
palace	mehal
park	bāğ
restaurant	"restaurant"
ruins	khanḍar
school	iskūl

shop	**dūkān**
stadium	**"stadium"**
statue	**mujasama**
Hindu temple	**mandir**
theater	**theṭar**
tomb	**maqbirā**
tower	**minārā**
university	**"university"**
zoo	**cuṛya-ghar**

—Occasions

birth	**paidā'ish**
death	**maut**
funeral	**janāza**
marriage	**shādī**

Holidays & festivals...

ISLAMIC (movable public holidays) — Since the date of Muslim festivals is based on the Muslim lunar calendar, they move in relation to the Western solar calendar, so you may want to ask around to be sure of the exact days they occur. The most important date in the Muslim calendar is **Ramzān** (Ramadan), the month of fasting. During Ramadan everyday life and work schedules slow down, and during daylight hours stores and restaurants close. Major feast days are: **Id-al-Fitr** which marks the end of Ramadan and fasting; and three months later, Muslims celebrate **Id-al-Haj**, which is when people traditionally come back from their pilgrimage to Mecca. **Mawlid**, the birthday of the prophet Muhammad, is also an important day for all Muslims. A big festival for Shi'i Muslims is **Ashūra**, which features an enactment of the martyrdom of Hussein, Muhammad's grandson, and in which devout followers beat themselves with whips. Another holiday is the Islamic New Year.

STATE HOLIDAYS — The following are fixed public holidays Pakistan Day (23 March); Labor Day (1 May); Independence Day (14 August); Defence of Pakistan Day (6 September); Anniversary of the Death of Qaid-i-Azam (11 September); Birthday of Allama Iqbal (National Poet) (9 November); Birthday of Qaid-i-Azam (25 December). Christmas Day and Boxing Day are celebrated by Christians only and are not public holidays.

12. FINANCE

> **CURRENCY** — The national currency of Pakistan is the **rūpīa** or rupee (abbreviated as "Rs"). This is divided into 100 **paisa**. Bills come in denominations of 1, 2, 5, 10, 50, 100, 500, and 1,000 rupees. When using credit cards the most widely accepted is American Express, followed by Visa and Mastercard, although in most places you will be expected to pay in cash. Take traveler's checks in U.S. dollars or pounds sterling. These can be changed by most banks and more upscale hotels. Always make sure you have enough small change when you are out and about, since large notes often can't be changed. Also, you'll find that people can be very fussy about torn and damaged bills and may well refuse to take them.

I want to change some dollars.	**Maiṅ apne ḍālar badalnā cāhtā hūṅ.**
I want to change some euros.	**Maiṅ apne euro badalnā cāhtā hūṅ.**
I want to change some pounds.	**Maiṅ apne pā'unḍ badalnā cāhtā hūṅ.**
Where can I change some money?	**Maiṅ paise kahāṅ badal saktā hūn?**
What is the exchange rate?	**Tabdīl karne kā ret kyā hai?**
Could you please check that again?	**Is phir se caik kaṛye?**
Could you please write that down for me?	**Āp mere liye likh sakte haiṅ?**
dollar	**ḍālar**
euro	**euro**
ruble	**ruble**
pound (sterling)	**pā'unḍ (sterling)**

a = apple. **ā** = father. **e** = pay. **i** = sit. **ī** = heat. **o** = hotel. **u** = put. **ū** = shoot. **au** = oar. **ai** = pay.

banknotes	**baink ke not**
calculator	**"calculator"**
cashier	**"cashier"**
coins	**sikke**
credit card	**"credit card"**
commission	**"commission"**
exchange	**tabdīl karnā** *or* **"exchange"**
loose change	**chuṭṭe**
receipt	**rasīd̤**
signature	**dastaxat**

WHEN TO VISIT — This depends on which region you visit. In the southern part of the country, outside the cooler months between November and April, it gets uncomfortably hot. In the northern mountainous regions it is best to go between May and October. After this point the snow sets in, and either disrupts or prevents travel altogether. It is certainly best to avoid the month of Ramadan when the Muslim population fasts during the daylight hours. The pace of life is seriously disrupted and many businesses close. However, some of the main restaurants and hotels will rustle up a meal to non-Muslims. Since the exact dates of Ramadan are based on the Muslim lunar calendar and move a few days every year in relation to the Western calendar, check before you leave.

13. COMMUNICATIONS

—Post

Where is the post office?	**"Post office" kahāṅ hai?**
What time does the post office open?	**"Post office" kitne baje khultā hai?**
What time does the post office close?	**"Post office" kitne baje band hotā hai?**
Where is the mail box?	**Xat post karne kā daba kahāṅ hai?**
Is there any mail for me?	**Mere līye ko'ī ḍāk hai?**
How long will it take for this to get there?	**Us ko āne meṅ kitnā vaqt lage gā?**
How much does it cost to send this to . . . ?	**Is ko . . . bhejne meṅ kitnā paisa lage?**
I would like some stamps.	**Mujhe kuch dāk tikiṭ cāhīye.**
I would like to send this to . . .	**Maiṅ ye . . . bhejnā cāhtā hūṅ.**
air mail	**air mail**
envelope	**lifā-fa**
mailbox	**dāk kā ḍabba**
parcel	**parsel**
registered mail	**"registered" dāk**
stamp	**dāk tikiṭ**
telegram	**"telegram"** *or* **tār**

—Tele-etiquette

I would like to make a phone call.	**Maiṅ fon karnā cāhtā hūṅ.**
I would like to send a fax.	**Maiṅ faiks karnā cāhtā hūṅ.**

a = *apple*. **ā** = *father*. **e** = *pay*. **i** = *sit*. **ī** = *heat*. **o** = *hotel*. **u** = *put*. **ū** = *shoot*. **au** = *oar*. **ai** = *pay*.

I would like to send a telex.	**Maiṅ ṭailaiks karnā cāhtā hūṅ.**
Where is the telephone?	**Fon kahāṅ hai?**
May I use your phone?	**Maiṅ āp kā fon istimāl kar saktā hūṅ?**
Can I telephone from here?	**Maiṅ yahāṅ se fon istimāl kar saktā hūṅ?**
Can you help me find this number?	**Āp is nambar ko ḍhūnḍne meṅ merī madad kar sakte haiṅ?**
Can I dial direct?	**Maiṅ dā'iraikt fon kar saktā hūṅ?**
May I speak to Mr . . . ?	**Maiṅ . . . Sāhib se bāt kar saktā hūṅ?**
May I speak to Ms/Mrs . . .?	**Maiṅ . . . Sāhiba/ Begam se bāt kar saktā hūṅ?**
Can I leave a message?	**Maiṅ peām choṛ saktā hūṅ?**
Who is calling, please?	**Kon bol rahā hai?**
Who are you calling?	**Āp kise fon kar rahe haiṅ?**
What is your name?	**Āp kā nām kyā hai?**
Which number are you dialing?	**Āp konsā nambar dā'il karnā cāhte haiṅ?**
He/She is not here.	**Vo is vaqt yahāṅ nahīṅ hai.**
Would you like to leave a message?	**Āp peām choṛnā cāhte haiṅ?**
This is not . . .	**Ye . . . nahīn hai.**
You are mistaken.	**Āp ğaltī per haiṅ.**
This is the . . . office.	**Ye . . . kā āfis hai.**

Hello, I need to speak to . . .	**Maiṅ . . . se bāt karnā cāhtā hūṅ.**
Sorry wrong number.	**Māf kaṛye, ğalat nambar hai.**
I want to call . . .	**Maiṅ . . . nambar dā'il karnā cāhtā hūṅ.**
What is the code for . . . ?	**. . . kā kod kyā hai?**
What is the international dialing code?	**International koḍ kyā hai?**
What do I dial for an outside line?	**Bāhar kī lā'in ke lī'ye kyā nambar dā'il karnā hai?**
The number is . . .	**Nambar . . . hai.**
The extension is . . .	**"Extension" . . . hai.**
It's engaged.	**Vo "engage" hai.**
The line has been cut off.	**Lā'in kat gā'ī hai.**
Where is the nearest public phone?	**Sab se qarībī pablik fon kahāṅ hai?**

—Phone words

digital	**"digital"**
e-mail	**"e-mail"**
extension (number)	**"extension"**
fax	**faiks**
fax machine	**faiks "machine"**
handset	**"handset"**
international operator	**"international operator"**
internet	**internet**
line	**"line"**
mobile phone	**"mobile phone"**
modem	**"modem"**
operator	**"operator"**
satellite phone	**"satellite phone"**

a = apple. **ā** = father. **e** = pay. **i** = sit. **ī** = heat. **o** = hotel. **u** = put. **ū** = shoot. **au** = oar. **ai** = pay.

telecommunications	**"telecommunications"**
telephone center	**"telephone center"**
telex	**teleks**
to transfer/put through	**"transfer" karne ke līye**

—Faxing & e-mailing

Where can I send a fax from?	**Maiṅ kahāṅ se faiks kar saktā hūṅ?**
Can I fax from here?	**Kyā maiṅ yehāṅ se faiks kar saktā hūṅ?**
How much is it to fax?	**Faiks karne kā kitnā paisā hogā?**
Is there an internet café here?	**Yehāṅ internait-kaife hai?**
Can I e-mail from here?	**Kyā maiṅ yehāṅ se "e-mail" kar saktā hūṅ?**
I know how to use this program.	**Mujhe ye progirām istimāl karna ātā hai.**
I don't know how to use this program.	**Mujhe ye progirām istimāl karna nahīṅ ātā hai.**
I want to print.	**Maiṅ pirint karnā cāhtā hūṅ.**

14. THE OFFICE

chair	**kursī**
computer	**"computer"**
desk	**"desk"**
drawer	**mez kā xāna**
fax	**faiks**
file *paper/computer*	**fā'il**
meeting	**mulāqāt**
paper	**kāğaz**
pen	**qalam**
pencil	**pensal**
photocopier	**zīroks mashīn**
photocopy	**zīroks kāpī**
printer	**"printer"**
(computer) program	**"program"**
report	**"report"**
ruler	**"ruler"**
scanner	**"scanner"**
telephone	**talifon**
telex	**teleks**
typewriter	**"typewriter"**

15. THE CONFERENCE

article *written*	**mazmūn**
a break for refreshments	**cā'e pānī kā vaqfā**
conference room	**"conference" kā kamrā**
copy	**"copy"**
discussion	**bāt-chīt**
forum	**"forum"**
guest speaker	**"guest speaker"** *or* **mehmān muqar-rir**
podium	**plaitfārm**
projector	**"projector"**
session	**nashist**
speaker	**muqar-rir**
subject	**mauzū**
to translate	**tarjumā kar**
translation	**tarjumā**
translator	**tarjumān**

16. ANIMALS

—Mammals

bat	**chamgadar**
bear	**bhalu**
boar	**jangli sūvar**
buffalo	**bhens**
bull	**ānḍ**
calf	**bachra**
camel	**unt**
cat	**billī**
cow	**gā'e**
deer	**hiran**
dog	**kuttā**
donkey	**gadhā**
elephant	**hāthī**
ewe	**bhair**
ferret	**neyvla**
flock	**rivāyatī**
fox	**lumri**
gazelle	**hiran**
goat	**bakrī**
herd	**ğol**
horse	**ghoṛā**
lamb	**dumbā**
leopard	**chitāh**
lion	**babar sher**
mare	**ghori**
mole	**chachondar**
monkey	**bandar**
mouse	**cūhā**
mule	**xaccar**
ox	**ba'el**
pig	**sūvar**
pony	**chota ghoṛā**

a = apple. **ā** = father. **e** = pay. **i** = sit. **ī** = heat. **o** = hotel. **u** = put. **ū** = shoot. **au** = oar. **ai** = pay.

rabbit	**xargosh**
ram	**bheṛa**
rat	**cūhā**
sheep	**bheṛ**
squirrel	**gila'ehri**
stallion	**nar ghoṛa**
tiger	**sher**
wolf	**gurg**

—Birds

bird	**parind**
chicken/hen	**murğī**
cock/rooster	**murğā**
crow	**kav-vā**
dove	**qumr**
duck	**batax**
eagle	**cīl**
falcon	**shahbaz**
goose	**gīz**
hawk	**uqab**
nightingale	**bulbul**
owl	**ullū**
parrot	**tota**
partridge	**chikor**
peacock	**mor**
pigeon	**kabutar**
quail	**bater**
rooster	**murğā**
sparrow	**chirya**
turkey	**turkī murğī**
vulture	**gidh**

—Insects & amphibians

ant	**coṅṭī**
bee	**shehad kī makh-khī**
butterfly	**titlī**

caterpillar	**kīṛā** *or* **tidda**
cobra	**nāg**
cockroach	**"cockroach"**
crab	**kekra**
cricket	**jhingar**
dragonfly	**bhan bairi**
fish	**machlī**
flea(s)	**pissū**
fly	**kīṛā**
flies	**kīṛe**
frog	**meṅḍak**
grasshopper	**jhingar**
hedgehog	**kharpusht**
hornet	**bhir**
insect	**kīṛā** *or* **makoṛā**
lizard	**chipkalī**
louse/lice	**jūṅ**
mosquito	**machchar**
scorpion	**bichu**
snake	**sāṅp**
spider	**makṛī**
termite	**dīmak**
tick	**saneha**
viper	**zehrila sanp**
wasp	**bhir**
worm	**ilī**

17. COUNTRYSIDE

canal	**nehar**
cave	**ğār**
dam	**band; bandh**
desert	**registān**
earthquake	**zal-zalā**
fire	**āg**
flood	**sailāb**
foothills	**pahāṛī**
footpath	**fotpath**
forest	**jangal**
glacier	**barfāni darya**
hill	**pahāṛ**
lake	**jhīl**
landslide	**"landslide"** *or* **zamīn kā khisaknā**
mountain	**pahāṛ**
mountain pass	**pahāṛī rāstā**
peak	**cotī**
plain/plains	**maidānī ilāqa**
plant	**podā**
range/mountain range	**pahāṛī silsila**
ravine	**khā'ī**
river	**nadī**
river bank	**nadī kā kināra**
rock	**caṭṭān**
slope	**ḍha'lān**
stream	**cashmā**
summit	**cotī**
swamp	**daldalī ilāqa**
tree	**jhāṛ**
valley	**vādī**
waterfall	**ābshār**
a wood	**lakṛī**

18. WEATHER

Pakistan has a variety of different climate zones. The northern part of the North Western Frontier Province is dominated by the spectacular mountain ranges of the Himalayas, the Karakorams and the Hindukush. During the winter months the mountains become snowbound, while in the foothills and highlands the summers are pleasant although winters get chilly. Summers in the Punjab and the southern region of the North Western Frontier can get extremely hot outside November and February. Meanwhile the Sindh in the south, with its desert regions, registers some of the highest temperatures in the world. During the spring and fall the valleys of Baluchistan enjoy cool and pleasant weather but the winters can be extremely cold, displaying a contrast with summer temperatures of more than 50 degrees centigrade. Most rain in Pakistan falls during the monsoon season that lasts from July to September.

What's the weather like?	**Mausam kaisā hai?**
The weather is . . . today.	**Āj mausam . . . hai?**
cold	**sard**
cool	**sardī** *or* **ṭhandī**
fresh	**tāzā**
cloudy	**abar-ālūd**
freezing	**barfīlī**
hot	**garam**
misty	**kuhar-ālūd**
very hot	**bohut garam**
windy	**havā'ī** *or* **tūfānī**
It's going to rain.	**Bārish hone vālī hai.**
It is raining.	**Bārish ho rahī hai.**
It's going to snow.	**Baraf paṛne vālī hai.**
It is snowing.	**Baraf paṛ rahī hai.**
It is very sunny.	**Bohut dhūp hai.**
air	**havā**
cloud	**bādal**

a = apple. **ā** = father. **e** = pay. **i** = sit. **ī** = heat. **o** = hotel. **u** = put. **ū** = shoot. **au** = oar. **ai** = pay.

3. INTRODUCTIONS

What is your name?	**Ism-e sharīf?***
My name is . . .	**Mujhe . . . kahte haiṅ.**
This is my . . .	**Ye mere . . . haiṅ.**
friend	**dost**
colleague	**kām ke sāthī**
companion	**sāthī**
relative	**rishte dār**

MR. & MRS. — Titles like **Sāhib** "Mr." and **Sāhiba** "Mrs./Miss" are more commonly used than in English and generally placed after the person's name, e.g. **Fred Sāhib**, **Emma Sāhiba**. **Begam** is another word for "Mrs./Miss" and is placed before the name, e.g. **Begam Emma**. Polite ways of addressing people when you do not know their names include **Janāb** "Sir," and **Begam Sāhiba** "Madam."

—Nationality

Pakistan	**Pākistān**
—Pakistani	**—Pākistānī**

Where are you from?	**Āp kahāṅ se haiṅ?****
I am from . . .	**Maiṅ . . . se hūṅ.**
America	**America**
Australia	**Australia**
Britain	**Batrāniya**
Canada	**Canada**
China	**Chīn**
England	**England**
Europe	**Europe**
France	**France**
Germany	**Germany**

* This translates literally as "(Your) good name?" A more literal way of asking this is: **Āp kā nām kyā hai?** "What is your name?" – response: **Merā nām . . . hai.** "My name is . . ."
** A polite way of asking this is as follows: **Āp kā ta'aluq kahāṅ se hai?** "Where are you from?" – **Maiṅ Inglaiṇḍ kā hūṅ.** "I'm from England."

India	**Hindūstān**
Iran	**Iran**
Ireland	**Ireland**
Ireland	**Italy**
Japan	**Japan**
the Netherlands	**Holland**
New Zealand	**New Zealand**
Scotland	**Scotland**
Spain	**Spain**
the USA	**USA**
Wales	**Wales**

I am . . .	**Maiṅ . . . hūṅ.**
American	**Amrīkī**
Australian	**Austṛailiā'ī**
British	**Bratānvī**
Canadian	**Canadian**
Dutch	**Dutch**
English	**Angrez**
French	**Fransisī**
German	**German**
Indian	**Hindustānī**
Iranian	**Irānī**
Irish	**Irish**
Israeli	**Israelī**
Italian	**Itālvī**
Portuguese	**Porchgīzī**
Scottish	**Scottish**
Spanish	**Hispānvī**
Welsh	**Welsh**

Where were you born?	**Āp kahāṅ paidā hūve?**
I was born in . . .	**Maiṅ . . . . meṅ paidā hūvā thā.**

a = apple. **ā** = father. **e** = pay. **i** = sit. **ī** = heat. **o** = hotel. **u** = put. **ū** = shoot. **au** = oar. **ai** = pay.

frost	**baraf**
full moon	**pūrā cānd**
hot wind	**garam havā**
ice	**baraf**
moon	**cānd**
new moon	**nayā cānd**
rain	**bārish**
season	**mausam**
snow	**baraf**
star	**cānd**
summer	**garmī'āṅ**
sun	**sūraj**
weather	**mausam**
winter	**sardī'āṅ**

More on clothing...

Although western clothes are worn in the big cities, everywhere in Pakistan local dress is the norm, especially since it is closely bound up with the rituals and sensibilities of Islam. In many parts of Pakistan both men and women wear a **qamīz**, a loose long shirt that reaches down below the knees, and **shalvār**, a type of baggy trousers — collectively known internationally as "shalwar-qameez" (**shalvār-qamīz**). In many areas men, especially the Pathans of the North Western Frontier Province, can be seen wearing a **paggri**, a type of cap. The turban is also seen in many areas, especially amongst the Punjabi.

Women all around the country will be seen wearing a **dupaṭṭā**, a light scarf that covers the head and shoulders. In some communities such as that of the Pathans, who observe strict Islamic codes, women in the more rural areas can be seen in "burqas," tent-like garments that cover the whole body and head.

Pakistan also has a long and rich tradition in the art of embroidery. The Sindh region is especially famous for its wonderfully embroidered dresses and the use of pieces of colored glass and mirrors sewn on to fabrics.

19. CAMPING

Where can we camp?	**Ham kahāṅ kaimp kar sakte haiṅ?**
Is it safe to camp here?	**Yahāṅ kaimp karnā mehfūz hai?**
Is there danger of wild animals?	**Yahāṅ per jaṅglī jānvaroṅ kā xatra hai?**
Is there drinking water?	**Yahāṅ pīne kā panī hai?**
May we light a fire?	**Ham āg jalā sakte haiṅ?**

—Kit

axe	**kulhāṛī**
bucket	**bālṭī**
campsite	**kaimp karne kī jagā**
can opener	**dabba kholne kī cābī**
compass	**"compass"**
firewood	**jalāne kī lakṛī**
gas canister	**gais kā dabba**
hammer	**hathoṛī**
ice axe	**baraf kātne kī kudāl**
lamp	**lamp** *or* **lālṭain**
mattress	**gadda**
penknife	**chota cāqū**
rope	**rasī**
sleeping bag	**"sleeping bag"**
stove	**"stove"**
tent	**"tent"** *or* **shāmiyāna**
water bottle	**panī kī boṭal**

a = apple. **ā** = father. **e** = pay. **i** = sit. **ī** = heat. **o** = hotel. **u** = put. **ū** = shoot. **au** = oar. **ai** = pay.

20. EMERGENCY

COMPLAINING — If you really feel you have been cheated or misled, raise the matter first with your host or the proprietor of the establishment in question, preferably with a smile. Urdus are proud but courteous, with a deeply felt tradition of hospitality, and consider it their duty to help any guest. Angry glares and shouting will get you nowhere.

CRIME — Pakistanis are both law-abiding and God-fearing people, but petty crime does occur. Without undue paranoia, take the usual precautions: watch your wallet or purse, securely lock your equipment and baggage before handing it over to railway or airline porters, and don't leave valuables on display in your hotel room. If you are robbed, contact the police. Of course in the more remote areas, sensible precautions should be taken, and always ensure that you go with a guide. In general, follow the same rules as you would in your own country and you will run little risk of encountering crime.

WHAT TO DO IF YOU LOSE SOMETHING — Save time and energy by appealing only to senior members of staff or officials. If you have lost items in the street or left anything in public transport, it is unlikely you will retrieve it.

DISABLED FACILITIES — The terrain and conditions throughout most of Pakistan do not make it easy for disabled visitors, particularly those in wheelchairs, to get around even at the best of times. Access to most buildings in the towns and cities is difficult, particularly since the majority of elevators function irregularly and ramps are rare. Facilities are not always available in hotels, airports or other public areas. However, human assistance will always be offered wherever you go and people will go to great lengths to help out, sometimes to the point of overkill.

TOILETS — You will find public utilities located in any important or official building. You may use those in hotels or restaurants. You may sometimes encounter failed plumbing and absence of toilet paper. Similar to Turkey and countries in the Middle East and North Africa, many people find it more hygienic to use water from a conveniently positioned tap or jug instead of toilet paper.

—Help expressions

Help!	**Madad!**
Could you help me, please?	**Āp merī madad kar sakte haiṅ?**

c = *church.* **ṅ** = *sing.* **x** = *loch.* **ğ/q** *see p18.* **bh/ch/dh/ḍh/gh/kh/ph/ṛh/th/ṭh** = *breathed.* **ḍ/ṛ/ṭ** = *flapped.*

Do you have a telephone?	**Āp ke pās fon hai?**
Can I use your telephone?	**Maiṅ āp kā fon istīmāl kar saktā hūṅ?**
Where is the nearest telephone?	**Qarībī fon kahāṅ hai?**
Does the phone work?	**Ye fon kām kartā hai?**
Get help quickly!	**Jaldī se madad bulā'īye!**
Call the police!	**Polīs ko bulā'īye!**
I'll call the police!	**Maiṅ polīs ko bulā'oṅ gā!**
Is there a doctor near here?	**Yahāṅ qarīb meṅ ḍākṭar hai?**
Call a doctor.	**Ḍāktar ko bulā'o.**
Call an ambulance.	**Ambulance ko bulā'o.**
Where is the doctor?	**Ḍāktar kahāṅ hai?**
Where is the hospital?	**Aspatāl kahāṅ hai?**
Where is the pharmacy?	**Davā'ī kī dūkān kahāṅ hai?**
Where is the dentist?	**Dāṅt kā ḍākṭar kahāṅ hai?**
Where is the police station?	**Polīs isṭeshan kahāṅ hai?**
Take me to a doctor.	**Mujhe ḍākṭar ke pās lejā'īye.**
There's been an accident!	**Vahāṅ per hadisa hūvā hai!**
Is anyone hurt?	**Ko'ī zaxmī hai?**
This person is hurt.	**Ye shaxs zaxmī hai.**
There are people injured.	**Vahāṅ per log zaxmī haiṅ.**
Don't move!	**Mat hilye!**
Go away!	**Jā'īye!**

a = apple. **ā** = father. **e** = pay. **i** = sit. **ī** = heat. **o** = hotel. **u** = put. **ū** = shoot. **au** = oar. **ai** = pay.

I am lost.	**Maiṅ gum geā hūṅ.**
I am ill.	**Maiṅ bīmār hūṅ.**
I've been robbed.	**Mujhe lūt liyā geā hai.**
Thief!	**Cor, cor!**
My . . . has been stolen.	**Merā/Mere . . . corī ho ga'ī hai/haiṅ.**
I have lost . . .	**. . . gum geā/ga'ī hai.**
my bags	**merā beg**
my camera	**merā kaimrā**
my handbag	**merā chotā beg**
my laptop computer	**merā "laptop computer"**
my money	**mere paise**
my passport	**merā pāsporṭ**
my traveler's checks	**mere ṭravlarz cheks**
my wallet	**merā pars**
I have a problem.	**Mujhe aik mushkil hai.**
Forgive me.	**Mujhe māf kaṛye.**
I speak English.	**Maiṅ Angrezī boltā hūṅ.**
I need an interpreter.	**Mujhe tarjumān kī zarūrat hai.**
Where are the toilets?	**Paxāne kahāṅ hai?**

c = *church*. **ṅ** = *sing*. **x** = *loch*. **ğ/q** *see p18*. **bh/ch/dh/ḍh/gh/kh/ph/ṛh/th/ṭh** = *breathed*. **ḍ/ṛ/ṭ** = *flapped*.

21. HEALTHCARE

INSURANCE — Medical insurance is a must. Make sure your policy covers Pakistan and read the small print carefully to make sure that it covers any hazardous activity or sports you are planning to do.
MALARIA — Malaria does occur in parts of Pakistan but check with your doctor before leaving home to see what, if any, anti-malarial drug you ought to take. Ask him or her about the potential side effects of the available drugs before deciding on which you might need to take.
CHEMISTS/PHARMACIES — These are easy to find but can be understocked at times. Don't forget to check the "best before" date. If planning to travel off the beaten track, it is probably best to bring a sufficient supply of any specific medication you require.

What's the trouble?	**Kyā taklīf hai?**
I am sick.	**Maiṅ bīmār hūṅ.**
My companion is sick.	**Merā sāthī bīmār hai.**
May I see a female doctor?	**Maiṅ "lady doctor" se milnā cāhtī hūṅ?**
I have medical insurance.	**Mere pās tibbī inshorains hai.**
Please undress.	**Patā batā'īye.**
How long have you had this problem?	**Ye taklīf kitne din se hai?**
How long have you been feeling sick?	**Āp ko taklīf kitne din se hai?**
Where does it hurt?	**Kahāṅ taklīf hai?**
It hurts here.	**Yahāṅ taklīf hai.**
I have been vomiting.	**Mujhe qe ā rahī hai.**
I feel dizzy.	**Mujhe cakkar ā rahā hai.**
I can't eat.	**Maiṅ khā nahīn saktā** *(m)*/**saktī** *(f)*.

a = apple. **ā** = father. **e** = pay. **i** = sit. **ī** = heat. **o** = hotel. **u** = put. **ū** = shoot. **au** = oar. **ai** = pay.

I can't sleep.	**Maiṅ so nahīn saktā** *(m)*/**saktī** *(f)*.
I feel worse.	**Merī tabīyat bohut xarāb hai.**
I feel better.	**Ab tabīyat ṭhīk hai.**
Do you have diabetes?	**Āp ko diabetes hai?**
Do you have epilepsy?	**Āp ko mirgī hai?**
Do you have asthma?	**Āp ko dama hai?**
I have diabetes.	**Mujhe "diabetes" hai.**
I have epilepsy.	**Mujhe mirgī hai.**
I have asthma.	**Mujhe dama hai.**
I'm pregnant.	**Maiṅ hāmila hūṅ.**

—Diagnosis

I have . . .	**Mujhe . . . hai.**
You have . . .	**Āp ko . . . hai.**
a cold	**zukām** *or* **sardī**
a cough	**balğam** *or* **khāṅsī**
a headache	**sar-dard**
a pain	**dard** *or* **taklīf**
a sore throat	**sūja galā**
a temperature	**buxār**
an allergy	**"allergy"**
an infection	**"infection"**
an itch	**khujlī**
backache	**kamar kā dard**
constipation	**qabz**
diarrhea	**pecish**
fever	**buxār**
hepatitis	**"hepatitis"** *or* **pīlia**
indigestion	**bad-hazmī**
influenza	**"influenza"**
a heart condition	**dil kī bīmarī**

pins and needles	**cūṅtiyān reṅgne kī taklīf**
stomach ache	**paiṭ kā dard**
a fracture	**frakshā**
toothache	**dāṅt kā dard**
I take this medication.	**Maiṅ ye davā letā hūṅ.**
I need medication.	**Mujhe is davā kī zarūrat hai.**
What type of medication is this?	**Ye kaisī davā hai?**
How many times a day must I take it?	**Din meṅ kitnī bār ye lenā hai?**
How long must I take it?	**Kab tak ye lenā hai?**
I'm on antibiotics.	**Maiṅ "antibiotics" per hūṅ.**
I'm allergic to . . .	**Mujhe . . . se ailargī hai.**
I do not need a vaccine.	**Mujhe vaiksīn kī zarūrat nahīṅ hai.**
I have my own syringe.	**Mere pās apna "syringe" hai.**
Is it possible for me to travel?	**Mere līye safar karnā mumkin hai?**

—Health words

AIDS	**AIDS**
alcoholic	**sharābī**
alcoholism	**sharāb kī ādat**
amputation	**kātnā**
anemia	**"anemia"**
anesthetic	**"anesthetic"** *or* **be hoshī ki davā**

a = apple. **ā** = father. **e** = pay. **i** = sit. **ī** = heat. **o** = hotel. **u** = put. **ū** = shoot. **au** = oar. **ai** = pay.

anesthetist	**"anesthetist"**
antibiotic	**"antibiotic"**
antiseptic	**"antiseptic"**
aspirin	**"aspirin"**
blood	**xūn**
blood group	**xūn kā grūp**
blood pressure:	
low blood pressure	**"low blood pressure"**
high blood pressure	**"high blood pressure"**
blood transfusion	**"blood transfusion"** *or* **xūn denā**
bone	**haḍḍī**
cancer	**"cancer"**
cholera	**haizā**
clinic	**"clinic"**
cold: head cold	**zukām**
dentist	**"dentist"** *or* **dāṅt kā ḍāktar**
diarrhea	**pecish**
drug (medical)	**davā**
drug (narcotic)	**manshīyāt**
epidemic	**vabā**
fever	**buxār**
food poisoning	**khane ki taklif**
I ate this food.	**Maiṅ ne ye khana kaya.**
flu	**buxār**
germs	**jarāsīm**
heart attack	**dil kā daurā**
heat stroke	**lū**
HIV	**"HIV"**
hygiene	**hifzān-e-sehat**
infection	**"infection"**
insect bite	**kīṛe kā kātā**
This insect bit me.	**Kīṛe ne mujhe kāta hai.**

c = *church.* **ṅ** = *sing.* **x** = *loch.* **ğ/q** *see p18.* **bh/ch/dh/ḍh/gh/kh/ph/ṛh/th/ṭh** = *breathed.* **ḍ/ṛ/ṭ** = *flapped.*

itching	**khujlī**
jaundice	**pīlī'ā**
limbs	**hāth-pā'oṅ**
malaria	**malerī'ā**
mosquito bite	**machchar kā kātā**
needle	**sū'ī**
nurse	**"nurse"**
operating theater/room	**"operating theater"**
(surgical) operation	**"operation"** *or* **jerāhī**
oxygen	**"oxygen"**
painkiller	**"painkiller"** *or* **dard kī davā**
physiotherapy	**"physiotherapy"**
rabies	**kutte ke kāṭne kī bīmārī**
rash	**khujlī**
sleeping pills	**sone kī golī**
smallpox	**cecak**
snake bite	**sāṅp kā kātā**
This snake bit me.	**Mujhe is sāṅp ne kātā hai.**
stethoscope	**"stethoscope"** *or* **ḍāktar kā āla**
sunstroke	**lū lagnā**
surgeon	**"surgeon"**
(act of) surgery	**amal-e-jerrahī**
syringe	**"syringe"**
thermometer	**"thermometer"**
tiredness	**thakāvaṭ**
tranquillizer	**behoshī kī davā**
venereal disease	**sozāk**
virus	**"virus"**
vomiting	**ulṭī**

a = apple. **ā** = father. **e** = pay. **i** = sit. **ī** = heat. **o** = hotel. **u** = put. **ū** = shoot. **au** = oar. **ai** = pay.

—Eyecare

I have broken my glasses.	**Merā gilās ṭūṭ geā hai.**
Can you repair them?	**Āp ise ṭhīk kar sakte haiṅ?**
I need new lenses.	**Mujhe na'e cashme kī zarūrat hai.**
When will they be ready?	**Ye kab teyār ho gā?**
How much do I owe you?	**Kitne paise denā hai?**
contact lenses	**"contact lenses"**
contact lens solution	**"contact lens solution""**

Some common expressions . . .

Here are a few expressions you'll hear in everyday conversation:

nā?	isn't it?/aren't they?/ aren't you? etc.
bas!	well now!; enough!
kyoṅ!	well!
to!	so!; indeed!
ya'nī!	I mean...; that is...
calī'e...!	come on...!
ṭhīk ṭhāk!	okay!
hai na?	isn't it?
ek minaṭ ṭhahrī'e!	wait a minute!
mere xayāl se...	in my opinion...
xair!	all right!
vāh!; shābāsh!	bravo!

22. TOOLS

binoculars	**dūr bīn**
brick	**īṅṭ**
brush	**"brush"**
cable	**tār**
cooker	**"cooker"**
drill	**"drill"**
eyeglasses	**cashma**
gas bottle	**gais kī botal**
hammer	**hathoṛa**
handle	**"handle"**
hose	**"hose"** *or* **baṛa pā'ip**
insecticide	**kīṛe mārne kī davā**
ladder	**sīṛhī**
machine	**"machine"**
microscope	**"microscope"**
nail	**nāxun**
padlock	**zanjīr kā tāla**
paint	**"paint"** *or* **roğan**
pickax	**kudāl**
plank	**ballī**
plastic	**"plastic"**
rope	**rasī**
rubber	**"rubber"**
saw	**ārī**
scissors	**qaiṅcī**
screw	**"screw"** *or* **paiṅc**
screwdriver	**paiṅc kas**
spade	**phā'oṛa**
spanner/wrench	**pāna**
string	**rasī**
sunglasses	**dhūp kā cashma**
telescope	**"telescope"**
varnish	**"varnish"** *or* **roğan**
wire	**tār**

a = apple. **ā** = father. **e** = pay. **i** = sit. **ī** = heat. **o** = hotel. **u** = put. **ū** = shoot. **au** = oar. **ai** = pay.

23. THE CAR

To drive in Pakistan you can use either an international or your own national driver's license. Don't forget to make sure that you have all the necessary documentation and are fully insured for the car you are driving. All drivers must be over 18 years old, or 21 if renting a car. There are several categories of roads including the major highways that link the major cities as well as recently constructed motorways on special routes. Bear in mind that each of these has its own speed limit, so check before driving. Most important — remember to drive on the left in Pakistan!

In some areas such as the Karakoram Highway that connects Pakistan with China, 4-wheel drives are recommended. If you plan to drive over the border with India or China be sure to check with the appropriate authorities for visa requirements and other necessary documentation. The Khujrab Pass leading into China is closed during the winter months and the only route into India, which is at Wagha, has strict summer and winter opening times. The key to an easier journey is to prepare well in advance rather than leave things to the last moment.

CAR RENTAL — Although the minimum driving age is 18, car rental companies will not rent to anyone under 21. Make sure the rental firm has provided you with comprehensive insurance for the car you are driving.

Where can I rent a car?	**Maiṅ kahāṅ kār kirā'e per le saktā hūṅ.**
With a driver?	**"Driver" ke sāth?**
How much is it per day?	**Ek din kā kitnā hogā?**
How much is it per week?	**Ek hafte kā kitnā hogā?**
Can I park here?	**Maiṅ yahāṅ pārk kar saktā hūṅ?**
Are we on the right road for. . . ?	**Kyā ham . . . ke līye sahī raste per haiṅ?**
Where is the nearest petrol station?	**Qarībī paiṭrol pamp kahāṅ hai?**

c = church. ṅ = sing. x = loch. ğ/q see p18. bh/ch/dh/ḍh/gh/kh/ph/ṛh/th/ṭh = breathed. ḍ/ṛ/ṭ = flapped.

Fill the tank please.	**Pūra ṭaink bhaṛye.**
Check the oil/tires/ battery, please.	**"Oil"/"tire"/"battery" caik kaṛye.**
I have lost my car keys.	**Merī kār kī cābī gum gā'ī hai.**
I've broken down.	**Merī kār xarāb ho gā'ī hai.**
There is something wrong with my car.	**Merī kār meṅ kuch gaṛ-baṛ hai.**
There is something wrong with this car.	**Is kār meṅ kuch gaṛ-baṛ hai.**
I have a puncture/ flat tire.	**Pancar ho geā hai.**
I have run out of petrol.	**Petrol xatam ho geā hai.**
Our car is stuck.	**Hamārī kār phaṅs gā'ī hai.**
We need a mechanic.	**Ham ko mekanik kī zarūrat hai.**
Can you tow us?	**Ham ko to kar sakte haiṅ?**
Where is the nearest garage?	**Qarībī gairāj kahāṅ hai?**
There's been an accident.	**Vahaṅ per hadisa hūvā hai.**
My car has been stolen.	**Merī kār corī ho gā'ī hai.**
Call the police!	**"Police" ko bulā'īye!**

a = apple. **ā** = father. **e** = pay. **i** = sit. **ī** = heat. **o** = hotel. **u** = put. **ū** = shoot. **au** = oar. **ai** = pay.

—Car words

> The majority of words relating to vehicles will be of direct English (generally British) origin and are readily understood, e.g. accelerator, battery, brake, driver, driver's license, engine, exhaust, fan belt, gear, indicator light, insurance policy, oil, oilcan, passenger, radiator. A few words with distinct translations or pronunciations follow below.

air	**havā**
clutch	**kilāc**
fender	**bāmpar**
gas	**petrol**
hood	**bānit**
jack	**jak**
mechanic	**mekanik**
neutral drive	**"neutral" meṅ calāna**
parking lot	**"car park"**
reverse	**rivās**
seat	**sīṭ**
speed	**spīḍ** *or* **raftār**
steering wheel	**"steering wheel"** *or* **hainḍal**
tank	**ṭānk**
tire/tyre	**tā'ir**
spare tire	**spe-tā'ir**
tow rope	**"tow" karne kī rasī**
trunk/boot	**būt** *or* **ḍikkī**
windshield/windscreen	**"windscreen"**
windshield wipers	**"windscreen wipers"**

24. SPORTS

Pakistan's national sport is hockey, but cricket enjoys an enormously popular following and its leading players are often treated as heroes. The crowning glory in Pakistan's history of cricket was when it won the 1992 World Cup. Pakistan also excels in squash and produces world champions. Football and basketball are also very popular.

athletics	**"athletics"**
ball	**bal**
basketball	**"basketball"**
chess	**shatranj**
cricket	**krikeṭ**
football *soccer*	**fuṭbāl**
goal	**gol**
golf	**golf**
hockey	**hokī**
horse racing	**ghore kī res**
horse riding	**ghorā savārī**
match	**mac**
pitch; playing field	**pic**
referee	**referi**
rugby	**rāgbī**
skiing	**ski'ing**
squash	**sikwāsh**
stadium	**staiḍiyam**
swimming	**tairnā**
team	**ṭīm**
tennis	**ṭanis**
wrestling	**paihilvānī**

Who won?	**Kon jītā?**
What's the score?	**Iskor kyā hai?**
Who scored?	**Kis ne iskor kyā?**

25. THE BODY

ankle	**taxnā**
arm	**bāzū**
back	**kamar**
beard	**dāṛhī**
blood	**xūn**
body	**jism**
bone	**haḍḍī**
bottom	**chūtaṛ**
breast/chest	**chātī**
chin	**ṭhuḍḍī**
ear	**kān**
elbow	**kuhnī**
eye	**āṅkh**
face	**cehrā**
finger	**unglī**
foot	**pā'oṅ**
genitals	**tanāsulī ā'zā**
hair	**bāl**
hand	**hāth**
head	**sar**
heart	**dil** *or* **qalb**
jaw	**jabṛā**
kidney	**gurdā**
knee	**ghuṭnā**
leg	**ṭāṅg**
lip	**hoṅṭ**
liver	**kalejī**
lung	**phepṛe**
mustache	**mūṅch**
mouth	**mūṅ**
neck	**gardan**
nose	**nāk**
shoulder	**kāndhā**

c = *church*. **ṅ** = *sing*. **x** = *loch*. **ğ/q** *see p18*. **bh/ch/dh/ḍh/gh/kh/ph/ṛh/th/ṭh** = *breathed*. **ḍ/ṛ/ṭ** = *flapped*.

stomach	**peṭ**
teeth	**dāṅt**
throat	**galā**
thumb	**aṅghūta**
toe	**pā'oṅ kā paṅja**
tongue	**zabān**
tooth	**dāṅt**
vein	**rag**
waist	**kamar**
womb	**bacca dānī**
wrist	**kalā'ī**

What to wear...

When deciding what clothes to pack, remember that Pakistan is a Muslim country and you should have regard for local sensibilities. Both men and women should avoid wearing shorts and women should wear long skirts or trousers and long-sleeved tops For business meetings and formal occasions men wear suits. With summer temperatures in everywhere but the far north reaching 100 degrees Fahrenheit or more, and little respite during the evenings, it is best to wear light cotton clothes. You could try wearing a "shalwar-qamiz," a combination of a long loose-fitting shirt and baggy trousers suitable for men and women. Around December and February daytime temperatures are often around 60 Fahrenheit or less and nights can be cold, so bring along warmer clothes, including sweaters. The far north enjoys pleasant summers, but winters are cold so take extra warm clothes. In high altitudes, mountain conditions apply, so be sure to get proper advice before venturing into these regions. The rainiest period in Pakistan is during the monsoon season between July and September, so be sure to have a raincoat or umbrella handy.

26. TIME & DATES

century	**sadī**
decade	**das sāl**
year	**sāl**
month	**mahīna**
week	**haftā**
day	**din**
hour	**ghanṭā**
minute	**minaṭ**
second	**sekond**
dawn	**sehr**
sunrise	**tulo āftāb**
morning	**subah**
daytime	**din kā vaqt**
noon/ afternoon	**dopehar**
evening	**shām**
sunset	**ğorūb āftāb**
night	**rāt**
midnight	**ādhī rāt**
four days before	**cār din pehle**
three days before	**tīn din pehle**
the day before yesterday	**parsoṅ**
yesterday	**kal**
today	**āj**
tomorrow	**kal**
the day after tomorrow	**persoṅ**
three days from now	**tīn din bād**
four days from now	**cār din bād**
last year	**pichle sāl**
this year	**is sāl**
next year	**agle sāl**

last week	**pichle hafte**
this week	**is hafte**
next week	**agle hafte**
this morning	**āj subah**
now	**abb**
tonight	**āj rāt**
yesterday morning	**kal subah**
yesterday afternoon	**kal dopehar ko**
yesterday night	**kal rāt ko**
tomorrow morning	**kal subah**
tomorrow afternoon	**kal dopehar ko**
tomorrow night	**kal rāt**
in the morning	**subah**
in the afternoon	**dopehar ko**
in the evening	**shām ko**
past	**māzī** *or* **pehle**
present	**hāzir** *or* **abb**
future	**mustaqbil**
What date is it today?	**Āj kyā tarīx hai?**

LANGUAGE TIP — **Kal** means both "yesterday" and "tomorrow", while **parsoṅ** means "the day before yesterday" and "the day after tomorrow." A mix of context and verb tense ensures the precise timing intended.

—Days of the week

Monday	**Pīr**
Tuesday	**Mangal**
Wednesday	**Budh**
Thursday	**Jumerāt**
Friday	**Jumā**
Saturday	**Hafta**
Sunday	**Itvār**

Two alternative day names are **Somvār** for Monday and **Sanīcar** for Saturday.

a = apple. **ā** = father. **e** = pay. **i** = sit. **ī** = heat. **o** = hotel. **u** = put. **ū** = shoot. **au** = oar. **ai** = pay.

—Months

January	**Janvarī**
February	**Farvarī**
March	**Mārc**
April	**Aprel**
May	**Mā'ī**
June	**Jūn**
July	**Julā'ī**
August	**Agast**
September	**Sitambar**
October	**Aktūbar**
November	**Navambar**
December	**Disambar**

—Islamic months

These months are based on the lunar calendar rather than the solar cycle used to calculate the Western calendar. **Ramzān** is the month when Muslims fast, **Zilhaj** when Muslims go on the **haj**, or pilgrimage to Mecca.

Muharram
Safar
Rabī-ul-Avval
Rabī-us-Sānī
Jamādī-ul-Avval
Jamādī-us-Sānī
Rajab
Sha'bān
Ramzān
Shavvāl
Zīqad
Zilhaj

—Time

What time is it?	**Kitne baje haiṅ?**
It is . . . o'clock.	**. . . baje haiṅ.**

27. NUMBERS

From 1 to 100, Urdu numbers have developed a unique form for each numeral, although there is still clearly an underlying decimal system.

0	**sifar**
1	**ek**
2	**do**
3	**tīn**
4	**cār**
5	**pāṅc**
6	**che**
7	**sāt**
8	**āṭh**
9	**no**
10	**das**
11	**giyāra**
12	**bāra**
13	**terā**
14	**codā**
15	**pandrā**
16	**solā**
17	**satrā**
18	**aṭhāra**
19	**unnīs**
20	**bīs**
21	**ikkīs**
22	**bāīs**
23	**teīs**
24	**caubīs**
25	**paccīs**
26	**chabbīs**
27	**satāīs**
28	**aṭhāīs**
29	**untīs**
30	**tīs**
31	**iktīs**
32	**battīs**
33	**taiṅtīs**
34	**cauṅtīs**
35	**paiṅtīs**
36	**chattīs**
37	**saiṅtīs**
38	**aṛtīs**
39	**untālīs**
40	**cālīs**
41	**iktālīs**
42	**beālīs**
43	**taiṅtālīs**
44	**cavālīs**
45	**paiṅtālīs**
46	**cheālīs**
47	**saiṅtālīs**
48	**aṛtālīs**
49	**uncās**
50	**pacās**

a = apple. **ā** = father. **e** = pay. **i** = sit. **ī** = heat. **o** = hotel. **u** = put. **ū** = shoot. **au** = oar. **ai** = pay.

51	**ikyāvan**	81	**ikyāsī**
52	**bāvan**	82	**beāsī**
53	**tirpan**	83	**tirāsī**
54	**cauvan**	84	**caurāsī**
55	**pacpan**	85	**pacāsī**
56	**chappan**	86	**cheāsī**
57	**satāvan**	87	**satāsī**
58	**aṭhāvan**	88	**aṭhāsī**
59	**unsaṭh**	89	**unanavve**
60	**sāṭh**	90	**navve**
61	**iksaṭh**	91	**ikyāṅve**
62	**bāsaṭh**	92	**beāṅve**
63	**tirsaṭh**	93	**tirāṅve**
64	**cauṅsaṭh**	94	**caurāṅve**
65	**paiṅsaṭh**	95	**pacāṅve**
66	**cheāsaṭh**	96	**cheāṅve**
67	**saṛsaṭh**	97	**satāṅve**
68	**aṛsaṭh**	98	**aṭhāṅve**
69	**unhattar**	99	**nināṅve**
70	**sattar**	100	**(ek) so**
71	**ikhattar**		
72	**bahattar**	200	**do so**
73	**tirhattar**	300	**tīn so**
74	**cauhattar**	400	**cār so**
75	**pachattar**	500	**pāṅc so**
76	**chihattar**	600	**che so**
77	**sathattar**	700	**sāt so**
78	**aṭhattar**	800	**āṭh so**
79	**unāsī**	900	**no so**
80	**assī**	1,000	**hazār**

10,000	**das hazār**	1,000,000	**milyūn**
50,000	**pecās hazār**	10,000,000	**karoṛ**
100,000	**(ek) lākh**	1,000,000,000	**arb**

first	**pehlā**
second	**dūsrā**
third	**tīsrā**
fourth	**cauthā**
fifth	**pāṅcvāṅ**
sixth	**chaṭṭā**
seventh	**sātvān**
eighth	**āṭhvān**
ninth	**navvān**
tenth	**dasvāṅ**
twentieth	**bīsvāṅ**
once	**ek bār**
twice	**do bār**
three times	**tīn bār**
one-half	**ādha**
one-third	**ek tihā'ī**
one-quarter	**ek cothā'ī**
two-thirds	**do tihā'ī**

—Weights & measures

kilometer	**kilomītar**
mile	**mīl**
meter	**mīter**
foot	**fot**
yard	**gaz**
gallon	**galan**
liter	**līter**
ton	**tan**
kilogram	**kilo**
pound	**pā'und**
gram	**gram**
ounce	**auns** *or* **chatāk**

a = apple. **ā** = father. **e** = pay. **i** = s*i*t. **ī** = heat. **o** = hotel. **u** = p*u*t. **ū** = shoot. **au** = oar. **ai** = pay.

28. OPPOSITES

beginning—end	**shurū'āt—xatam**
clean—dirty	**sāf—gandā**
happy—unhappy	**xush—nā-xush**
life—death	**zindagī—maut**
friend—enemy	**dost—dushman**
open—shut	**khol—band**
wide—narrow	**caur'ā—ṭang**
high—low	**oṅcā—nīcā**
peace—violence/war	**aman—tashaddud/jang**
silence—noise	**xāmūshī—shor-o-ğul**
cheap—expensive	**sastā—mahaṅgā**
hot/warm—cold/cool	**garam—ṭhanḍā**
health—disease	**sehat—bīmārī**
well—sick	**achchā—bīmār**
night—day	**rāt—din**
top—bottom	**ūpar—niche**
backwards—forwards	**pīche—āge**
back—front	**kamar—āge**
near—far	**qarīb—dūr**
left—right	**bāyāṅ—dāyaṅ**
in—out	**andar —bāhar**
up—down	**ūpar—nīce**
here—there	**yahāṅ—vahaṅ**
easy—difficult	**āsān—mushkil**
quick—slow	**jald—dhīre**
strong—weak	**mazbūt—kamzor**
success—failure	**kāmyābī—nākāmī**
young—old	**choṭā—barā**
new—old	**nayā—purānā**
question—answer	**savāl—javāb**
safety—danger	**hifāzat—xatrā**
true—false	**sac—jhūtā**
truth—lie	**saccā'ī—jhūṭ**

c = *church*. **ṅ** = *sing*. **x** = *loch*. **ğ/q** *see p18*. **bh/ch/dh/ḍh/gh/kh/ph/ṛh/th/ṭh** = *breathed*. **ḍ/ṛ/ṭ** = *flapped*.

MAP OF PAKISTAN

Punjabi-English/English-Punjabi Dictionary
25,000 entries • 426 pages • 5½ x 8½ •
0-7818-0940-1 • $19.95pb • (401)

Tajik-English/English-Tajik Dictionary & Phrasebook
3,000 entries • 226 pages • 3¾ x 7 •
0-7818-0662-3 • $11.95pb • (752)

English-Telugu Pocket Dictionary
12,000 entries • 386 pages • 5 x 7 •
0-7818-0681-X • $17.50hc • (952)

Turkish-English/English-Turkish Dictionary & Phrasebook
2,500 pages • 228 pages • 3¾ x 7½ •
0-7818-0904-5 • $11.95pb • (230)

Uzbek-English/English-Uzbek Dictionary & Phrasebook
3,000 entries • 200 pages • 3¾ x 7½ •
0-7818-0959-2 • $11.95pb • (166)

Uzbek-English/English-Uzbek Concise Dictionary
7,500 entries • 329 pages • 4 x 6 •
0-7818-0165-6 • $11.95pb • (4)

All prices are subject to change without prior notice. To order Hippocrene Books, contact your local bookstore, call (718) 454-2366, visit www.hippocrenebooks.com, or write to: Hippocrene Books, 171 Madison Avenue, New York, NY 10016. Please enclose check or money order adding $5.00 shipping (UPS) for the first book and $.50 for each additional title.